BUILDING VOCABULARY FOR COLLEGE

SECOND EDITION

R. Kent Smith

University of Maine, Bangor

D. C. Heath and Company
Lexington, Massachusetts   Toronto

Acquisitions Editor: Paul Smith

Developmental Editor: Holt Johnson

Production Editor: Cathy Labresh Brooks

Designer: Sally Thompson Steele

Production Coordinator: Lisa Arcese

Published simultaneously in Canada.

Printed in the United States of America.

International Standard Book Number: 0-669-20470-6

10 9 8 7 6 5 4 3 2 1

To the Instructor

This worktext is designed primarily for use in comprehensive secondary reading, writing, and study skills courses, although it is certainly suitable for courses devoted exclusively to vocabulary development. Relevant content and a practical strategy for learning the meaning of words characterize the text's three sections. The lesson exercises not only test but also foster an increasing familiarity with each word.

Section One is devoted to the study of Latin and Greek word elements that hold the key to understanding thousands of English words. Section Two is concerned with words college students should know for advanced reading. Section Three focuses on academic terms essential to the understanding of the basic concepts dealt with in college introductory courses. The word elements, words, and academic terms were selected after consulting college introductory textbooks, comprehensive and specialized dictionaries, vocabulary and reference books, and periodicals and professional journals, as well as college instructors and students.

Using contextual clues and examining word structure, the most practical methods of unlocking the meaning of unknown words, are emphasized in the first two sections. However, Section Three provides definitions similar to those found in textbook glossaries because students must know precise meanings of academic terms. The *Instructor's Guide* contains instructional suggestions, an answer key, and mastery tests.

As a college teacher, I am certainly aware of the positive correlation that exists between an extensive vocabulary and academic success. But I also realize how difficult it is to provide significant vocabulary instruction within the context of multi-purpose courses like reading, writing, and study skills. However, I trust that you will discover, as others have, that *Building Vocabulary for College*, Second Edition is practical, effective, and time-saving for both you and your students.

R. Kent Smith

Notes on the Second Edition

My own testing experience and the helpful advice I have received from other instructors led to these major changes in the second edition:

- *Section One: Word Parts* is doubled in size, with the ten lessons now including 100 affixes and roots.
- *Section Two: General Words* is reduced to twenty lessons, the 200 general words now grouped by part of speech and arranged in alphabetical order. In addition, each lesson's concluding exercise now probes for word mastery through using synonyms, antonyms, and analogies.
- In *Section Three: Academic Terms*, fifteen disciplines are now represented in twenty lessons. New categories include art, music, business, and economic terms.
- Appendixes A and B now include information concerning the dictionary and parts of speech.
- The *Instructor's Guide and Testing Program* features many more tests, with a mastery test now available after each group of twenty words or word elements. Pretests and posttests for each of the three sections are also included.

Acknowledgments

I am indebted to the following reviewers for their insightful suggestions for this second edition: Shirley A. Biggs, University of Pittsburgh; Terri Bruce, Kellogg Community College; Ann Fields, Western Kentucky University; Susan Fuqua, Volunteer State Community College; Lei Lani Hinds, Honolulu Community College; Harriet Johnson, Hunter College; Walter Klarner, Johnson County Community College; James R. Miller, North Texas State University; Judith Anne Moore, New Mexico State University—Carlsbad; Karen Pelz, Western Kentucky University; Shirley Quinn, Wellesley College; Thomas R. Schnell, University of Missouri—St. Louis.

I am also most appreciative to Stephanie Graves for her generous, gracious, and timely assistance. Thank you to my students and to my long-time colleague, Clayton Pinette, for their interest and valuable feedback.

Special thanks are due D. C. Heath editors Paul Smith, for initiating this second edition, and Cathy Labresh Brooks, for her intelligent and thorough guidance through every phrase of this project.

Finally, I wish to express my gratitude to my loved ones for their patience, interest, and good cheer: Barbara, Steve, Jan, Shawn, Laura, Jim, Emily, Gladys, Wayne, and Evie.

To the Student

It is difficult to overemphasize the value of developing an extensive vocabulary. Not only do we communicate in words, but also we do most of our thinking in words. As a college student, you will discover that familiarity with the vocabulary being used in a certain academic subject will determine your ability to grasp the concepts dealt with in lectures and textbooks.

No one is born with a better vocabulary than anyone else. Those who possess the advantages that come with an extensive vocabulary have made the necessary efforts to enlarge their knowledge of words. If you are willing to do likewise, the benefits of a broad vocabulary can be yours.

While it is true that most of the words you know were learned in a natural, incidental manner as you grew up, as an adult you must now make deliberate efforts to learn new words if you are to considerably increase your vocabulary. In fact, acquiring a college education will be easier if you make the special efforts necessary to enlarge your vocabulary.

This book gives you the opportunity to increase your vocabulary in a practical, comprehensive manner. Section One deepens your understanding of the meanings of common word parts—prefixes, suffixes, and roots. Knowledge of these word parts will help you to understand hundreds of words. Section Two helps you learn the definitions of many words that you will encounter in advanced reading, both in and out of college. Section Three presents important academic terms associated with subjects that you are likely to take in college.

Undoubtedly, you will already know the meanings of some of the words and word elements contained in this book. The meanings of others you will know vaguely; most, however, will probably be completely new to you. But regardless of your present situation, your vocabulary will increase significantly with conscientious work on your part. As a result, your speaking, writing, reading, listening, and thinking abilities will improve, and your ability to unlock the meanings of unfamiliar words will develop. Those accomplishments will certainly enhance your chances for academic success in college.

R. Kent Smith

Contents

Section Three: Academic Terms   187

Word Parts

The ten lessons in this section present you with an opportunity to master the meaning of common prefixes, suffixes, and roots. A knowledge of these word parts and a sensitivity to contextual clues, which is discussed in Section Two, will enable you to understand hundreds of difficult words.

A *prefix*, which is a word part added to the beginning of a word, dramatically alters the meaning of a word, often changing it to its opposite: correct, *in*correct; handle, *mis*handle. By understanding that the prefixes *mis-* and *in-* change words to their opposite, you possess an important key to comprehending words like *in*-discreet and *mis*nomer. So because of their significant impact on base words, prefixes are the most frequent word part studied in this section.

A *suffix*, which is a word part added at the end of a word, does not generally alter a word's meaning so dramatically as does a prefix, but it will often change a word from one part of speech to that of another: jump (verb), jump*er* (noun); poison (noun), poison*ous* (adjective). In addition, a suffix often provides a clue for understanding an academic term. For example, if you know that *-tion* signifies a noun and often expresses action, then you possess valuable clues for comprehending transpira*tion*, a biology term, particularly if you also understand the meaning of the prefix *trans-*.

A *root* is a basic word to which prefixes and suffixes can be added. For example, *path*, a root associated with feelings, can have the prefix *sym-* and the suffix *-ize* added to it to form sym*path*ize. And when you know the meaning of *path*, you can more easily learn words like *empathy* and *apathy*. Therefore, becoming familiar with the roots in Section One will make the learning of many words much easier.

To do the lessons, begin each by carefully reading the sentences that appear before the first exercise, paying particular attention to the word in italics. After you have read the two sample sentences for each word part, try to form a definition for it in your own words. Then do the first exercise, which requires you to match each word part to an appropriate definition. When you are satisfied that you have correctly matched the word parts to their definitions, proceed to the second exercise. This exercise requires you to complete a word with either a prefix, suffix, or root. There are times when word parts do not possess their usual meaning; in fact, they sometimes are not prefixes, suffixes, or roots at all. For example, the prefix *anti-* means "against" or "opposite of," as in anti*magnetic*. However, *anti-* is not a prefix in either *anticipate* or *antique*. Therefore, the third exercise in each lesson is devoted to testing your ability to make such distinctions.

The concluding exercise of each lesson requires you to write a definition for each prefix, suffix, or root studied in the lesson; then, with the help of a dictionary, if needed, you are to list words in which these word parts appear.

After you have completed all the exercises, your instructor will correct your work or make an answer key available to you. You should find the lessons in Section One challenging but relatively easy to do. Be assured, however, that the knowledge you gain about prefixes, suffixes, and roots will make valuable contributions to your immediate, as well as to your future, vocabulary growth.

Important: Be prepared for a mastery test after Lessons 2, 4, 6, 8, and 10 as well as a comprehensive posttest.

Word Parts: prefixes, roots

1. **anti**

   a. The scientist's watch is *antimagnetic*, so its accuracy is not affected by experiments involving magnetic fields.

   b. The development of *antibodies*, because of their effectiveness against harmful bacteria, has contributed significantly to the average life span.

2. **auto**

   a. Contrasted to a carriage pulled by a horse, a car seems to move by its own power; that is why a car is known as an *automobile*.

   b. Our furnace will *automatically* turn off if the temperature in the house falls below 62 degrees.

3. **bio**

   a. Books about Abraham Lincoln's life are still being written, even though there are more *biographies* published about him than about any other American.

   b. Faye is doing extremely well in *biochemistry*, a course concerned with the chemistry of living matter.

4. **chron**

   a. Ricardo has had a *chronic* backache since he fell while roller skating three weeks ago.

   b. Generally, history texts present material in *chronological* order.

5. **eu**

   a. Mr. Henderson gave the *eulogy* at the memorial service for the mayor.

   b. The seniors expressed their *euphoria* on graduation night by tossing their mortarboards high in the air.

6. **gram, graph**

   a. We completed the project by following the steps outlined in the *diagram*.
   b. The television star signed her *autograph* on the restaurant's menu.

7. **hetero**

   a. Words having the same spelling but having different pronunciation and meanings, such as *lead* (a metal) and *lead* (to conduct), are called *heteronyms*.
   b. Animals of this type are generally *heterochromatic*, that is, of mixed colors.

8. **homo**

   a. Words having the identical spelling and pronunciation but having different meanings, such as *bat* (a club) and *bat* (a flying mammal), are called *homonyms*.
   b. Animals of this type are generally *homochromatic*, that is, or one color.

9. **log**

   a. The *dialogue* between the two major characters in the play is hilarious.
   b. Jenny solved the problem by using a *logical* approach.

10. **meter, metr**

   a. A *barometer* measures atmospheric pressure.
   b. *Trigonometry* is a branch of mathematics concerned with the calculations of sides and angles of triangles.

EXERCISES FOR LESSON 1
Word Parts: prefixes, roots

I. *Directions:* Match each definition to the word part it defines.

_____	**1.** anti	**a.**	different
_____	**2.** auto	**b.**	time
_____	**3.** bio	**c.**	write
_____	**4.** chron	**d.**	word, study
_____	**5.** eu	**e.**	life
_____	**6.** gram, graph	**f.**	opposite, against
_____	**7.** hetero	**g.**	measure
_____	**8.** homo	**h.**	good, well
_____	**9.** log	**i.**	self
_____	**10.** meter, metr	**j.**	same, like

II. *Directions:* Selecting from the list below, write the proper word part in each space so that the appropriate word is formed.

anti	bio	eu	hetero	log
auto	chron	gram, graph	homo	meter, metr

1. The people on the bus trip were a _____geneous group, enjoying the same sites and activities.

2. Howard felt _____phoric about his job promotion.

3. The houses in our development are quite _____geneous in design, with ranch, split-level, and colonial types all represented.

4. College students have more _____nomy than high school students, so they must learn to be responsible for themselves.

5. The _____sphere is the part of the earth's crust, waters, and atmosphere that supports living organisms.

6. The young man appears to be _____social; he seldom goes any place if many other people will be there.

7. A hygro_____ measures the water vapor content in the atmosphere.

8. The term associated with correct spelling is ortho_____y.

9. My grandparents have kept a diary, which provides a _____icle of their life together.

10. The author provided an epi_____ue at the end of the book to explain what eventually happened to his friends.

III. *Directions:* Write *Yes* in the space if the word part retains the meaning it had in the previous exercises, *No* if it does not.

_____ 1. The *antique* desk was auctioned for over $1,000.

_____ 2. Pollination of a flower by its own pollen is known as *autogamy*.

_____ 3. Doctors often do *biopsies* to study the living tissues of patients.

_____ 4. A *chronoscope* is an instrument for measuring small time intervals.

_____ 5. Is an English person considered a *European*?

_____ 6. Although she's not my grandmother, I've always called her *Grammy*.

_____ 7. A *heterosexual* is attracted to those of the opposite sex.

_____ 8. When milk is blended into a uniform blend, it is said to be *homogenized*.

_____ 9. Before Mr. Wilkinson showed his slides of China, he delivered a *prologue* to explain why he had traveled to that country.

_____ 10. Do you know how to determine the *diameter* of this figure?

IV. *Directions:* Without referring to the preceding pages in this lesson, write the meaning of each word part. Then write a whole word containing the word part followed by the whole word's definition. Do not use any words included in this lesson; however, you can consult a dictionary. An example has been done for you.

	Word Part	Meaning	Whole Word	Definition
Example:	anti	against	antiseptic	A substance that combats harmful germs.
1.	anti			
2.	auto			
3.	bio			
4.	chron			
5.	eu			
6.	gram or graph			
7.	hetero			
8.	homo			
9.	log			
10.	meter or metr			

Word Parts: prefixes, roots

1. **mono**

   a. Didn't Alex look hilarious with that *monocle* in his eye?
   b. *Monogamy* is the custom in our country, so you'll have to be content with just one spouse.

2. **neo**

   a. I had played tennis only twice before, but, fortunately, my opponent was also a *neophyte*.
   b. Some people are critical of her *neoteric* painting style, but I consider her approach refreshingly modern.

3. **pan**

   a. Athletes from North, Central, and South America participated in the *Pan-American* games.
   b. Barbara's dream is to have a house on the coast with a *panoramic* view of the ocean.

4. **phil**

   a. My aunt qualifies as an *Anglophile* because she admires everything English.
   b. President Franklin Roosevelt loved stamp collecting; he was a *philatelist* all his adult life.

5. **phon**

   a. A specific speech sound is known as a *phoneme*.
   b. Our old *phonograph* still has a good sound.

6. **poly**

    a. Even if *polygamy* were allowed, don't you think one husband or wife is sufficient?

    b. Christy is quite a *polygot*; she can speak French, Italian, and Spanish as well as English.

7. **pseudo**

    a. Astrology is a *pseudoscience*, so you are foolish to believe in it.

    b. Many criminals use a *pseudonym* rather than their true name.

8. **sym, syn**

    a. At a *symposium*, several speakers share the responsibility for leading discussions.

    b. By *synthesizing* the information and clues revealed by the extensive investigation, the detective was able to solve the baffling crime.

9. **tele**

    a. Michael needs a more powerful *telescope* to see the most distant planets.

    b. This historic *telecast* was the first time people in all sections of the nation could witness a presidential inauguration.

10. **the**

    a. *Theology* is concerned with the study of God and religion.

    b. Yes, I'm a *theist*; don't you believe in a god?

EXERCISES FOR LESSON 2
Word Parts: prefixes, roots

I. *Directions:* Match each definition to the word part it defines.

_____	**1.** mono	**a.**	sound
_____	**2.** neo	**b.**	far
_____	**3.** pan	**c.**	God
_____	**4.** phil	**d.**	many
_____	**5.** phon	**e.**	one
_____	**6.** poly	**f.**	together, with
_____	**7.** pseudo	**g.**	love
_____	**8.** sym, syn	**h.**	all
_____	**9.** tele	**i.**	false
_____	**10.** the	**j.**	new

II. *Directions:* Selecting from the list below, write the proper word part in each space so that the appropriate word is formed.

mono	pan	phon	pseudo	tele
neo	phil	poly	sym, syn	the

1. The _____anthropist's concern and generosity were deeply appreciated by those left homeless after the fire.

2. _____ocracy is a form of government led by officials who are thought to be divinely guided.

3. A term used for harsh, discordant sounds is caco_____y.

4. Mr. Nickerson formed a _____dictate with some business associates to buy the trucking firms.

5. A term for a new word is _____logism.

6. By making it possible to send voices from distant places, the _____phone revolutionized communications.

7. The police were fearful that the large crowd would erupt into _____demonium when the concert was canceled.

8. A mineral that looks identical to another one but which does not actually contain the same composition is called a _____morph.

9. I would like to join the choir, but, unfortunately, I sing in a _____tone.

10. In geometry class, you will learn to construct and measure _____gons, which are figures having many angles.

III. *Directions:* Write *Yes* in the space if the word part retains the meaning it had in the previous exercises, *No* if it does not.

_____ 1. Peter complains that his job gets *monotonous* at times.

_____ 2. A *neoplasm*, generally called a tumor, is a new growth of tissue serving no physiological purpose.

_____ 3. The old dog was *panting* after chasing the squirrel across the lawn.

_____ 4. The LeFevres' *philanthropy* enabled the senior citizens' center to be built.

_____ 5. That's the *phoniest* excuse I've ever heard.

_____ 6. My cousin is attending a *polytechnical* school where you can study anything from computer science to automotive repair.

_____ 7. He tries to impress people with his knowledge, but he's really a *pseudointellectual*.

_____ 8. A *synthetic* product is made artificially through the joining of chemical elements or compounds.

_____ 9. Do you ever stop to think about what a remarkable invention *television* is?

_____ 10. The professor explained the *theory* on which his research is based.

IV. *Directions:* Without referring to the preceding pages in this lesson, write the meaning of each word part. Then write a whole word containing the word part followed by the whole word's definition. Do not use any words included in this lesson; however, you can consult a dictionary.

Word Part	Meaning	Whole Word	Definition
1. mono			
2. neo			
3. pan			
4. phil			
5. phon			
6. poly			
7. pseudo			
8. sym or syn			
9. tele			
10. the			

Word Parts: prefixes, roots

1. a, an

    a. Douglas is certainly *atypical* from his brothers; he doesn't enjoy hunting and fishing as they do.

    b. When the central government was overthrown, no one was able to enforce the laws, so complete *anarchy* reigned.

2. ad

    a. The radio announcer warned that the storm would *advance* to the coast by early morning.

    b. The *advent* of the holiday season meant that the Toys and Games Shoppe in the mall would experience its busiest time of the year.

3. ann, enn

    a. Our *annual* family reunion will be in Ohio this year.

    b. We look forward to our *perennial* flowers blooming every spring.

4. ante

    a. Harry Truman's presidency *antedates* John Kennedy's by eight years; between their terms in office, Dwight Eisenhower was president.

    b. A pronoun must refer to a previous noun. For example, in the sentence, "The *package* will be expensive to mail because *it* weighs more than eight pounds," *package* is the *antecedent* of the pronoun *it*.

5. bene

    a. As the result of a generous contribution from an unannounced *benefactor*, the college will be able to complete its building program.

    b. Hazel was the *beneficiary* of her aunt's insurance policy, so she can now afford to open a florist shop of her own.

6. **bi**

    a. The United States' *bicentennial* in 1976 celebrated the country's two-hundredth anniversary.

    b. One of my neighbors has been accused of *bigamy*; apparently, his divorce was not finalized before he remarried.

7. **cap**

    a. Anwar was elected *captain* of the team.

    b. Madison is the *capital* city of Wisconsin.

8. **co, col, com, con, cor**

    a. In an impressive display of civic pride, the downtown merchants *cooperated* when they remodeled their storefronts.

    b. Three of my friends *collaborated* in finishing the project.

    c. Tad Phillips, my *companion* in the navy, is now a dentist in South Dakota.

    d. George Washington and Benjamin Franklin were *contemporaries*.

    e. Norma wasn't surprised when the doctor told her that her coughing was *correlated* to her smoking.

9. **contra, contro, counter**

    a. She *contradicted* what Wanda had told me.

    b. The *controversy* was about who was responsible for paying the bill.

    c. Our troops rallied in the afternoon and launched a *counterattack*.

10. **cred**

    a. Monique is an honest person, so I know she will be a *credible* witness.

    b. Have you always subscribed to that religious *credo* or *creed*?

EXERCISES FOR LESSON 3
Word Parts: prefixes, roots

I. *Directions:* Match each definition to the word part it defines.

_____	**1.** a, an	**a.** year
_____	**2.** ad	**b.** good, well
_____	**3.** ann, enn	**c.** believe, trust
_____	**4.** ante	**d.** with, together
_____	**5.** bene	**e.** opposed to
_____	**6.** bi	**f.** to, toward
_____	**7.** cap	**g.** before, in front of
_____	**8.** co, col, com, con, cor	**h.** two
		i. not, without
_____	**9.** contra, contro, counter	**j.** head, chief
_____	**10.** cred	

II. *Directions:* Selecting from the list below, write the proper word part in each space so that the appropriate word is formed.

a, an	ann, enn	bene	cap	counter
ad	ante	bi	col, con	cred

1. The article begins with a _____tion that summarizes the major points the author discusses.

2. Dr. Morton's _____room was filled with patients.

3. The _____ibility of the candidate suffered when it was discovered that he had exaggerated his scholastic achievements.

4. An _____onymous person telephoned my parents to complain about the way I drive my car in the neighborhood.

5. Rosaria used her _____noculars to get a more detailed look at the impressive mountains.

6. Our community church celebrated its cent_____ial last July.

7. The doctor _____curred with his _____league's diagnosis.

8. Victoria's _____vancement to the top of her profession came as no surprise because she is intelligent and hardworking.

9. Smoking is certainly _____productive to your otherwise good health practices.

10. Doyle's advice has proved _____ficial to many people.

III. *Directions:* Write *Yes* in the space if the word part retains the meaning it had in the previous exercises, *No* if it does not.

_____ 1. Sally decided to *adopt* the kitten that she had found.

_____ 2. Mr. Chang receives an *annuity* from his investment the first of every year.

_____ 3. Many people experience *anxiety* when they go to the dentist.

_____ 4. An *anteater* is certainly an odd looking animal.

_____ 5. Antonio found an old ring *beneath* a rock in his garden.

_____ 6. My sister and I used to play *bingo* with our grandparents.

_____ 7. The marvelous announcement *captured* everyone's interest.

_____ 8. All the houses in the new development must *conform* to the same architectural design.

_____ 9. Today's weather is quite a *contrast* from yesterday's, isn't it?

_____ 10. I wouldn't put too much *credence* in that story, if I were you.

IV. *Directions:* Without referring to the preceding pages in this lesson, write the meaning of each word part. Then write a whole word containing the word part followed by the whole word's definition. Do not use any words included in this lesson; however, you can consult a dictionary.

	Word Part	Meaning	Whole Word	Definition
1.	a, an			
2.	ad			
3.	ann, enn			
4.	ante			
5.	bene			
6.	bi			
7.	cap			
8.	choose one: co, col, com, con, cor			
9.	choose one: contra, contro, counter			
10.	cred			

Word Parts: prefixes, roots

1. de

    a. She filed a grievance because of her *demotion* in rank.

    b. The trees that had been toppled by storms through the years were in various stages of *decomposition*.

2. dis

    a. Logan had been working long hours, but that's no excuse for his being *discourteous* to the customers.

    b. The Chiefs will be at a *disadvantage* in the game because their star player is injured.

3. em, en

    a. Do you trust the lawyer who has been *empowered* to act for grandmother?

    b. The coach *encouraged* Tiffany to try out for the team.

4. equ

    a. Many people *equate* expensive cars with wealth.

    b. Needless to say, tightrope walkers must have good *equilibrium*.

5. ex

    a. The dentist had to *extract* the patient's badly decayed tooth.

    b. Oranges are a major *export* of California and Florida.

6. extra, ultra

    a. It was *extraordinary* for Miami to be so cool in March.

    b. Mr. Michaels is an *ultraconservative*; he doesn't believe in federal support for education or in treaties with foreign countries.

7. **fid**

    a. Marjorie *confided* to Brian that she was engaged because she knew he wouldn't tell anyone else.

    b. My stereo has such good *fidelity* that you would swear that the music was being played live in my room.

8. **il, im, in, ir**

    a. In some communities, it is *illegal* for businesses to be open on Sundays.

    b. Skip was so stiff and sore from playing football that he was practically *immobile*.

    c. The people in the photograph were so *indistinct* that I couldn't identify anyone.

    d. The judge dismissed the evidence as *irrelevant*.

9. **mal**

    a. The *malicious* gossip destroyed her chances of winning the election.

    b. The doctor was shocked when she was charged with *malpractice*.

10. **man**

    a. Jess did *manual* work all summer, so he felt fit and strong when he reported for football practice in the fall.

    b. His hands and fingernails needed a *manicure*.

EXERCISES FOR LESSON 4
Word Parts: prefixes, roots

I. *Directions:* Match each definition to the word part it defines. (One definition is used twice.)

_____	**1.** de	**a.**	equal
_____	**2.** dis	**b.**	out, outside
_____	**3.** em, en	**c.**	bad, evil
_____	**4.** equ	**d.**	faith, trust
_____	**5.** ex	**e.**	put into
_____	**6.** extra, ultra	**f.**	not, opposite of
_____	**7.** fid	**g.**	hand
_____	**8.** il, im, in, ir	**h.**	down, away from, separation
_____	**9.** mal	**i.**	beyond, extreme
_____	**10.** man		

II. *Directions:* Selecting from the list below, write the proper word part in each space so that the appropriate word is formed.

de	em, en	ex	fid	mal
dis	equ	extra, ultra	in	man

1. The earth is divided into hemispheres at the _____ator.

2. It is important to have con_____ence in your doctor.

3. An _____competent mechanic attempted to repair my car.

4. He was accused of _____ipulating the records to cover his fraud.

5. Unfortunately, a great amount of _____ice exists between the couple filing for divorce.

6. Cars _____preciate quite rapidly in value.

7. Steve snored every time he _____haled.

8. Congress _____acted the bill into law last month.

9. The puppy was trying to _____entangle himself from the chain.

10. The Olympic Games are a wonderful _____vaganza to witness.

III. *Directions:* Write *Yes* in the space if the word part retains the meaning it had in the previous exercises, *No* if it does not.

_____ 1. Make sure you put the *decimals* in the right location.

_____ 2. The team played with poise and *discipline*.

_____ 3. The woodwork was painted in white *enamel*.

_____ 4. Phil's motorcycle is *equipped* with all types of gadgets.

_____ 5. The general public is *excluded* from certain areas of the White House.

_____ 6. The scientist indicated that the *ultraviolet* rays were responsible for the photo's fine details.

_____ 7. The *affidavit* required that his testimony be factual and complete.

_____ 8. It was *irresponsible* of Daryl not to carry an extra set of car keys on our trip.

_____ 9. We were *formally* introduced to the officers of the club.

_____ 10. The original *manuscript* of the *Declaration of Independence* still exists.

IV. *Directions:* Without referring to the preceding pages in this lesson, write the meaning of each word part. Then write a whole word containing the word part followed by the whole word's definition. Do not use any words included in this lesson; however, you can consult a dictionary.

Word Part	Meaning	Whole Word	Definition
1. de			
2. dis			
3. em, en			
4. equ			
5. ex			
6. extra, ultra			
7. fid			
8. il, im, in, ir			
9. mal			
10. man			

Word Parts: prefixes

1. hyper

   a. Gail is *hyperactive*, so she often jogs to use up her excess energy.

   b. Be tactful when you offer your suggestions to Alex because he is *hypersensitive*.

2. hypo

   a. A *hypodermic* needle is a needle inserted under the skin.

   b. The patient has *hypotension*, which is the opposite of high blood pressure.

3. inter

   a. Our team plays a number of *intercollegiate* basketball games with colleges from the Midwest.

   b. A network of *interstate* highways links all sections of our country.

4. mis

   a. A run scored when the shortstop *misplayed* the ball.

   b. The cylinders in my car are *misfiring*.

5. multi

   a. A *multitude* of people were crowded in front of the courthouse.

   b. It was a *multinational* meeting, with representatives from as far away as Finland and China.

6. non

   a. Kate is a *nonconformist*, so she has trouble with those in authority.

   b. I'm a *nonpartisan*, so I don't care which political party wins the election.

7. ob, op

   a. The lawyer's objection to the witness's testimony was overruled by the judge.

   b. The Huskies should be tough *opponents* for the Bruins.

8. **omni**

   a. Young children often believe that their parents are *omniscient*, but, as they grow older, they realize that their parents don't know everything after all.

   b. Dogs seem to be *omnipresent* at picnics.

9. **path**

   a. The newspaper's picture of the *pathetic* orphan brought offers of adoption.

   b. The movie was full of *pathos*, and many people in the audience cried.

10. **peri**

    a. Frank's not sure of the exact *perimeter* of the property his father owns, but he knows it embraces nearly 250 acres.

    b. The commander ordered the *periscope* raised so that he could get a complete view of the submarine's surroundings.

EXERCISES FOR LESSON 5
Word Parts: prefixes

I. *Directions:* Match each definition to the word part it defines.

_____	**1.** hyper	**a.** wrong
_____	**2.** hypo	**b.** against
_____	**3.** inter	**c.** not
_____	**4.** mis	**d.** feelings
_____	**5.** multi	**e.** less, under, insufficient
_____	**6.** non	**f.** all
_____	**7.** ob, op	**g.** between, among
_____	**8.** omni	**h.** around
_____	**9.** path	**i.** many
_____	**10.** peri	**j.** over, too much

II. *Directions:* Selecting from the list below, write the proper word part in each space so that the appropriate word is formed.

hyper	inter	multi	ob, op	path
hypo	mis	non	omni	peri

1. The movie star claims he was _____quoted by the reporter.

2. A _____patetic person is one who travels about a great deal.

3. Sheila overcame many _____stacles to graduate from college.

4. The president of the company considered himself to be _____potent, so he was angered when the board of directors questioned a number of his decisions.

5. We were able to understand because she explained the basic concept in _____technical language.

6. Harry appreciated his friends' expressions of sym_____ y when they learned of his grandfather's death.

7. The doctor prescribed medicine for the patient's _____tension, better known as high blood pressure.

8. We noticed several _____ dermic needles on the beach.

9. The audience was served refreshments during the _____ lude between the first and second acts.

10. The wallpaper is _____ colored, including shades of blue, red, green, and brown.

III. *Directions:* Write *Yes* in the space if the word part retains the meaning it had in the previous exercises, *No* if it does not.

_____ 1. Laboratory tests are being performed to find the cause of the water's *hyperacidity.*

_____ 2. A stage of development in which something is much smaller than expected is known as *hypoplasia.*

_____ 3. Isabella will be an *intern* in Seattle starting in July.

_____ 4. Because Waldo made so many *mistakes,* he was fired from his job.

_____ 5. Where are we going to store this *multivolume* set of encyclopedias?

_____ 6. Sweden is a *nonaligned* nation, so it refused to support either country during the war.

_____ 7. The Johnsons are taking their dog to *obedience* school.

_____ 8. My dog is *omnivorous*; he'll eat anything!

_____ 9. After his girlfriend broke up with him, Russell was not interested in anything, and his *apathy* upset his parents.

_____ 10. We subscribed to a number of *periodicals,* including *Time* and *Newsweek.*

IV. *Directions:* Without referring to the preceding pages in this lesson, write the meaning of each word part. Then write a whole word containing the word part followed by the whole word's definition. Do not use any words included in this lesson; however, you can consult a dictionary.

Word Part	Meaning	Whole Word	Definition
1. hyper			
2. hypo			
3. inter			
4. mis			
5. multi			
6. non			
7. ob, op			
8. omni			
9. path			
10. peri			

Word Parts: prefixes, roots

1. pos

    a. Lucia was promoted to a managerial *position*.

    b. During the museum's remodeling, paintings were stored in a *repository*.

2. post

    a. At the conclusion of the wedding ceremony, Barbara played an original *postlude* on the organ.

    b. Ludwig added a *postscript* to his letter because he had forgotten to include the exact time his plane would be arriving.

3. pre

    a. We saw a *preview* of next week's movie at the Student Union.

    b. The staff *prearranged* the room for the banquet, so the guests were able to be seated immediately.

4. pro

    a. My folks have always been *promusic*, so they are delighted I'm taking guitar lessons.

    b. Mr. Simpson, who often complains about the property taxes he has to pay, surprised me when he became a leading *proponent* for a new community swimming pool.

5. re

    a. Mrs. Lucas had to *revarnish* the table after it was stained by candle drippings.

    b. The Warners had such a good vacation in British Columbia that they hope to *revisit* this Canadian province next year.

6. **semi**

   a. A *semicolon* is part colon and part comma (;).
   b. We arranged our chairs in a *semicircle*, but after more people arrived, we made a complete circle.

7. **spec**

   a. My husband always *inspects* our car carefully before we take a trip.
   b. The *spectators* at the air show were awed by the precision flying.

8. **sub**

   a. Although my parents live near the airport, they are not bothered by sonic booms because all planes must travel at *subsonic* speeds.
   b. As we watched the dark water, the monster slowly began to *submerge*.

9. **super**

   a. Tyrone is a *supervisor* at the auto plant.
   b. This new housing code *supersedes* the previous one.

10. **ten**

    a. The Blancos are among the *tenants* of the new building on the corner of Oak and Main Streets.
    b. Students held in *detention* at the high school I attended had to sit quietly for an hour and do homework.

EXERCISES FOR LESSON 6
Word Parts: prefixes, roots

I. *Directions:* Match each definition to the word part it defines.

_____	1. pos	a.	to look
_____	2. post	b.	under
_____	3. pre	c.	above, over
_____	4. pro	d.	place
_____	5. re	e.	after
_____	6. semi	f.	again
_____	7. spec	g.	to hold
_____	8. sub	h.	half of
_____	9. super	i.	before
_____	10. ten	j.	for, in favor of

II. *Directions:* Selecting from the list below, write the proper word part in each space so that the appropriate word is formed.

pos	pre	re	spec	super
post	pro	semi	sub	ten

1. The candidate's voting record reveals that he's _____labor on most issues, so he should get the support of the industrial states.

2. The scuba divers discovered a _____terranean tunnel on the south side of the isolated island.

3. Mr. Feliciano's _____ure as mayor was twelve years, the longest anyone in our community has held that office.

4. Would it be an im_____ition for you to drive me to work?

5. We are guilty of _____ judice when we make judgments before knowing all the facts.

6. The famous violinist gave another _____lative performance.

7. The sculptor, who had died during the year, was awarded the prize _____humously.

8. People included in the study were examined _____ annually, in January and July.

9. Marcia went back to the restaurant to _____trieve her raincoat and umbrella.

10. Ralph admits that, in retro_____t, he was wrong about the matter.

III. *Directions:* Write *Yes* in the space if the word retains the meaning it had in the previous exercises, *No* if it does not.

_____ 1. Where can we *dispose* of the garbage?

_____ 2. We must take care of the environment for *posterity.*

_____ 3. I will have to have my suit *pressed* before I wear it again.

_____ 4. The VCR is *programmed* to turn on at 10:00 P.M.

_____ 5. Because of smoke damage, the Hubbells had to *repaint* their kitchen walls.

_____ 6. The doctor sees patients only three days a week since he *semiretired.*

_____ 7. Why do you think Carla is so *special*?

_____ 8. The *subsoil* of our garden is as hard as a rock.

_____ 9. She was promoted to *superintendent* of schools.

_____ 10. In quartets, it is usually the *tenor* who holds the melody throughout the song.

IV. *Directions:* Without referring to the preceding pages in this lesson, write the meaning of each word part. Then write a whole word containing the word part followed by the whole word's definition. Do not use any words included in this lesson; however, you can consult a dictionary.

Word Part	Meaning	Whole Word	Definition
1. pos			
2. post			
3. pre			
4. pro			
5. re			
6. semi			
7. spec			
8. sub			
9. super			
10. ten			

Word Parts: prefixes, roots

1. **ambi, amphi**

   a. Miguel demonstrated his *ambidexterity* by first writing with his right hand and then with his left.

   b. An *amphibian*, such as a frog, can live on land or in water.

2. **aud**

   a. Because Olivia was suffering from a bad cold, her voice was barely *audible*.

   b. The *auditorium* was almost empty even though the program was scheduled to begin in fifteen minutes.

3. **dia**

   a. The length of a straight line through the center of a figure is the *diameter*.

   b. The *diastolic* reading is obtained when the blood is passing through the heart's chambers.

4. **dic**

   a. Norman's *diction* was influenced by his childhood years in England.

   b. Mr. Reed's *dictation* was concerned with the sales campaign.

5. **fin**

   a. The project should be *finished* by the first of October.

   b. What was the *final* score?

6. **fore**

   a. I had a *foreboding* that our team would lose the game and, sure enough, they did.

   b. Our *forefathers* established a republican form of government.

7. **gen**

   a. A motel he built fifteen years ago was the *genesis* of his financial empire.
   b. The child was operated on to correct a *congenital* problem with her spine.

8. **intra, intro**

   a. *Intrastate* commerce refers to business transactions within a state.
   b. *Introverts* are people primarily concerned with their own thoughts and feelings.

9. **macro, magni**

   a. The entire universe is sometimes referred to as a *macrocosm*.
   b. By using a *magnifying* glass, Ellen was able to read the message.

10. **mor, mort**

   a. Her business had been in a *moribund* condition for some time, so I'm not surprised that she declared bankruptcy.
   b. Mr. Wolfe is a *mortician*.

EXERCISES FOR LESSON 7
Word Parts: prefixes, roots

I. *Directions:* Match each definition to the word part it defines.

_____	1. ambi, amphi	a.	through
_____	2. aud	b.	death
_____	3. dia	c.	hear, listen
_____	4. dic	d.	birth, beginning
_____	5. fin	e.	large, great
_____	6. fore	f.	say, tell
_____	7. gen	g.	end, limit
_____	8. intra, intro	h.	before
_____	9. macro, magni	i.	both
_____	10. mor, mort	j.	inside, within

II. *Directions:* Selecting from the list below, write the proper word part in each space so that the appropriate word is formed.

ambi, amphi	dia	fin	gen	magni
and	dic	fore	intra, intro	mort

1. A _____tator exercises absolute control; his or her word becomes the law of the land.

2. Athletic contests among students attending the same institution are referred to as _____mural sports.

3. _____bious planes can land on land or water.

4. All living things are _____al; their days are numbered.

5. The first book in the Bible is _____esis.

6. A _____ficent cathedral covered the entire block.

7. It was a _____gone conclusion that they would marry soon after graduation.

8. The _____ience sat in rapt attention.

9. A _____gonal path had been worn in the grass leading from the post office to the bank.

10. We left immediately after the orchestra's _____ale.

III. *Directions:* Write *Yes* in the space if the word part retains the meaning it had in the previous exercises, *No* if it does not.

_____ 1. Leila's *ambition* is to become a successful novelist.

_____ 2. *Auditions* for the new television show are scheduled for the next two months.

_____ 3. I would have loved to have heard the *dialogue* that must have passed between these two old enemies.

_____ 4. It's colder than the *dickens* outside.

_____ 5. My daughter has always been a *finicky* eater.

_____ 6. Perspiration glowed on his *forehead*.

_____ 7. Our hereditary characteristics are determined by our *genes*.

_____ 8. Ronald became *introspective* listening to the music, and he was soon lost in his own thoughts.

_____ 9. It's a minor problem, so let's not *magnify* it out of proportion.

_____ 10. Fortunately, the *mortgage* rate was reasonable when we purchased our home.

IV. *Directions:* Without referring to the preceding pages in this lesson, write the meaning of each word part. Then write a whole word containing the word part followed by the whole word's definition. Do not use any words included in this lesson; however, you can consult a dictionary.

Word Part	Meaning	Whole Word	Definition
1. ambi, amphi			
2. audi			
3. dia			
4. dic			
5. fin			
6. fore			
7. gen			
8. intra, intro			
9. macro, magni			
10. mort			

Word Parts: prefixes, roots

1. **se**

   a. Mr. Artesani's photographs were *selected* for first prize.
   b. South Carolina became the first state to *secede* from the Union.

2. **temp**

   a. *Tempo* refers to the speed at which a musical passage is played.
   b. Angela will be a *temporary* replacement for Mr. Colville.

3. **terr**

   a. This is the best farming *territory* in the entire state.
   b. Firm, solid land is sometimes referred to as *terra firma*.

4. **therm**

   a. Jason set the *thermostat* on 62 degrees.
   b. The *thermometer* indicated that the temperature was below freezing.

5. **trans**

   a. Miriam plans to *transfer* to a college in Colorado.
   b. Trucks were used to *transport* the potatoes to market.

6. **un**

   a. The defense lawyer contended that the accident was caused by the
   weather, so she feels it would be *unjust* to make her client pay damages.
   b. The cows wandered out of the pasture when the gate was left *unlatched*.

7. **uni**

   a. Everyone said in *unison*, "Let's go!"
   b. This clock is *unique*; it is the only one ever made of bamboo.

8. **ver**

    a. Can you *verify* that this wallet is yours?

    b. Frankly, we doubted his story; however, the *veracity* of his statements was substantiated.

9. **vid, vis**

    a. The class was shown a *video* about the Everglades.

    b. Although some things are *invisible*, they are real, nevertheless.

10. **voc, vok**

    a. A *convocation* was called by the bishops to discuss the controversial issue.

    b. The unexpected letter *evoked* memories of her old friend.

EXERCISES FOR LESSON 8
Word Parts: prefixes, roots

I. *Directions:* Match each definition to the word part it defines.

_____ **1.** se	**a.** land, earth
_____ **2.** temp	**b.** true
_____ **3.** terr	**c.** to see, provide
_____ **4.** therm	**d.** one
_____ **5.** trans	**e.** across, change to
_____ **6.** un	**f.** to call, voice
_____ **7.** uni	**g.** apart from, away
_____ **8.** ver	**h.** heat
_____ **9.** vid, vis	**i.** time
_____ **10.** voc, vok	**j.** not

II. *Directions:* Selecting from the list below, write the proper word part in each space so that the appropriate word is formed.

se	terr	trans	uni	vid, vis
temp	therm	un	ver	voc

1. Fortunately, the window was still _____ broken after it suddenly slammed shut.

2. Can you en_____ ion what you'll be doing five years from now?

3. The Gardners are living _____ orarily in an apartment on Elm Street.

4. The photographs provided _____ ification that Christy had indeed won the race.

5. The _____ ain was obviously too rocky for either farming or grazing.

6. It was difficult to find Rick because all the men were wearing _____ forms.

7. The minister's in_____ ation began the chapel service.

8. I decided to _____plant the bush to a different location.

9. _____odynamics is concerned with the relationships between heat and the mechanical energy of work.

10. Andy longed for the _____clusion of his farm after experiencing the hustle and bustle of the city.

III. *Directions:* Write *Yes* in the space if the word part retains the meaning it had in the previous exercises, *No* if it does not.

_____ **1.** Bob *searched* everywhere for his billfold.

_____ **2.** Because of the great weather, I was *tempted* to skip class and go to the beach.

_____ **3.** The old house was in *terrible* condition.

_____ **4.** The workers wore *thermal* underwear to protect themselves from the bitter cold.

_____ **5.** The Bible has been *translated* into many languages.

_____ **6.** It was *unnecessary* for me to water the garden because of the morning's rain.

_____ **7.** Have you ever tried to ride on a *unicycle*?

_____ **8.** Henry displayed a lot of energy and *verve* on the dance floor.

_____ **9.** The flight was canceled because of poor *visibility*.

_____ **10.** Frank Sinatra became a popular *vocalist* in the 1940s.

IV. *Directions:* Without referring to the preceding pages in this lesson, write the meaning of each word part. Then write a whole word containing the word part followed by the whole word's definition. Do not use any words included in this lesson; however, you can consult a dictionary.

Word Part	Meaning	Whole Word	Definition
1. se			
2. temp			
3. terr			
4. therm			
5. trans			
6. un			
7. uni			
8. ver			
9. vid, vis			
10. voc, vok			

Word Parts: prefixes, roots

1. **anthrop**

   a. *Anthropology* involves the study of the origins, beliefs, and cultural development of humankind.
   b. He really seems to hate everyone; has he always been a *misanthrope?*

2. **astro**

   a. John Glenn, who is now a senator from Ohio, was among the first American *astronauts*.
   b. *Astrophotography* is concerned with photography of stars and other celestial objects.

3. **bell**

   a. A *rebellion* erupted in the capital city.
   b. My enjoyment of the hockey game was undermined by the *bellicose* behavior of some of the players; their fighting spoiled an otherwise good contest.

4. **bon, boun**

   a. Caroline received a *bonus* for exceeding the yearly sales quota.
   b. The wheat farmers are expecting a *bounteous* harvest next month.

5. **geo**

   a. *Geography* involves the study of the earth's surface, climate, population, and natural resources.
   b. *Geochemistry* is the study of the earth's composition and chemical changes.

6. **hemo**

    a. The protein matter of the red blood cells that carries oxygen throughout the body is called *hemoglobin*.

    b. *Hemophilia* is a condition in which the blood fails to clot.

7. **hydro**

    a. *Hydrology* is concerned with the distribution and properties of the earth's water supply.

    b. A *hydraulic* lift operates by fluid pressure.

8. **iso**

    a. *Isobars* are the lines drawn on weather maps to connect points that have equal atmospheric pressure.

    b. The *isograph* indicates areas of the country where a common dialect is spoken.

9. **mega**

    a. A *megaton* bomb is equal to the explosive force of one million tons of TNT.

    b. A type of mental illness characterized by delusions of greatness is termed *megalomania*.

10. **psych**

    a. *Psychosis* is a general term used to indicate a severe mental disorder or disease.

    b. A *psychosomatic* problem is a physical disorder caused by the mind or emotions.

EXERCISES FOR LESSON 9
Word Parts: prefixes, roots

I. *Directions:* Match each definition to the word part it defines.

_____	1. anthrop	a.	earth
_____	2. astro	b.	good
_____	3. bell	c.	mind, spirit
_____	4. bon, boun	d.	star
_____	5. geo	e.	large, great
_____	6. hemo	f.	war
_____	7. hydro	g.	equal
_____	8. iso	h.	water
_____	9. mega	i.	man, human
_____	10. psych	j.	blood

II. *Directions:* Selecting from the list below, write the proper word part in each space so that the appropriate word is formed.

anthrop	bell	geo	hydro	mega
astro	bon, boun	hemo	iso	psych

1. _____electric power is generated by water.

2. Mingson won the cash prize, which was quite a _____anza for her.

3. A _____lopolis is a region containing many large cities.

4. The science that is concerned with rocks and other aspects of the physical history of the earth is _____logy.

5. The artist must have painted this _____edelic picture when he was hallucinating!

6. Objects having equal measure are called _____metric.

7. A heavy discharge of blood is called a _____rrhage.

8. _____oids are animals, such as apes, that resemble humans.

9. Citizens are re_____ing because of the dictator's repression of personal freedom.

10. _____logy is a false science that professes to foretell the future by the positions of the stars and other heavenly bodies.

III. *Directions:* If the word parts and words opposite each are similar in meaning, write *Yes* in the space; if they are unrelated, *No*.

_____ 1. anthrop   man

_____ 2. astro   water

_____ 3. bell   noise

_____ 4. bon, boun   new

_____ 5. geo   earth

_____ 6. hemo   small

_____ 7. hydro   star

_____ 8. iso   alone

_____ 9. mega   immense

_____ 10. psych   mind

IV. *Directions:* Without referring to the preceding pages in this lesson, write the meaning for each word part. Then write a whole word containing the word part followed by the whole word's definition. Do not use any words contained in this lesson; however, you can consult a dictionary.

Word Part	Meaning	Whole Word	Definition
1. anthrop			
2. astro			
3. bell			
4. bon, boun			
5. geo			
6. hemo			
7. hydro			
8. iso			
9. mega			
10. psych			

Word Parts: suffixes

1. able, ible

    a. Burke insists that all the organization's problems are *manageable*.

    b. The fiddlehead is an *edible*, fernlike plant.

2. dermis

    a. The outer layer of the skin is called the *epidermis*.

    b. The *ectodermis* is the outer tissue of an embryo, which is the early developmental stage of an organism.

3. er, or, ist

    a. My cousin is a *rancher* in Montana.

    b. Joseph was the *cantor* at Rachel's wedding ceremony.

    c. It is sometimes difficult to work for someone who is a *perfectionist*.

4. ful, ous

    a. A *frightful* tornado carried Dorothy's house away.

    b. The well water was found to be *poisonous*.

5. ism

    a. Novels concerned with *romanticism* have always been popular.

    b. The belief that there is no god is called *atheism*.

6. itis

    a. Jorge is sick with *bronchitis*.

    b. The doctor prescribed aspirin for the patient's *arthritis*.

7. less

    a. Raisa is a *fearless* skier.

    b. It was another beautiful, *cloudless* day in New Mexico.

8. **logy**

   a. *Sociology* is concerned with the systematic study of society.
   b. Maria is majoring in *zoology*, the branch of *biology* devoted to the animal kingdom.

9. **ness, tion**

   a. Mr. Lewis enjoys the *quietness* of the early morning hours.
   b. The American *Revolution* began in 1775.

10. **phobia**

    a. My best friend suffers from *claustrophobia*; he cannot bear to be in a small, enclosed space.
    b. Once Jared overcame *hydrophobia*, he enjoyed the water and learned to swim.

EXERCISES FOR LESSON 10
Word Parts: suffixes

I. *Directions:* Match each definition to the word part it defines.

_____	**1.** able, ible	**a.** without
_____	**2.** dermis	**b.** capable of, condition of (often forms an adjective)
_____	**3.** er, or, ist	**c.** study of
_____	**4.** ful, ous	**d.** person who
_____	**5.** ism	**e.** fear
_____	**6.** itis	**f.** skin
_____	**7.** less	**g.** full of
_____	**8.** logy	**h.** quality of, expressing action (often acts as a noun)
_____	**9.** ness, tion	**i.** inflammation
_____	**10.** phobia	**j.** belief, doctrine

II. *Directions:* Selecting from the list below, write the proper word part in each space so that the appropriate word is formed.

able, ible	er, or, ist	ism	less	ness, tion
derm	ful, ous	itis	logy	phobia

1. Psycho_____ is the most interesting subject I've studied so far in college.

2. Jennifer's headaches are caused by sinus_____.

3. The belief that conditions will improve is called optim_____; the belief that conditions will get worse is called pessim_____.

4. The patient felt immediate relief after the doctor administered a hypo_____ic injection.

5. Since Tim conquered his acro_____, he no longer is afraid to climb ladders.

6. Both of the candidates were the victims of venom_____ rumors.

7. A commo_____ broke out in the stands between the opposing fans.

8. Even though it was a gray, cheer_____ day, Monica was in good spirits.

9. Did the optometr_____ say that you need glasses?

10. This is the most dur_____ paint we've ever had on the house.

III. *Directions:* If the word parts and words opposite each are similar in meaning, write *Yes* in the space; if they are unrelated, write *No.*

_____ 1. able, ible   capable of, condition of (often forms adjective)

_____ 2. dermis   hair

_____ 3. er, or, ist   person who

_____ 4. ful, ous   against

_____ 5. ism   inflammation

_____ 6. itis   belief, doctrine

_____ 7. less   without

_____ 8. logy   study of

_____ 9. ness, tion   quality of (often forms a noun)

_____ 10. phobia   ability for

IV. *Directions:* Without referring to the preceding pages in this lesson, write the meaning of each word part. Then write a whole word containing the word part followed by the whole word's definition. Do not use any words contained in this lesson; however, you can consult a dictionary.

Word Part	Meaning	Whole Word	Definition
1. able, ible			
2. dermis			
3. er, or, ist			
4. ful, ous			
5. ism			
6. itis			
7. less			
8. logy			
9. ness, tion			
10. phobia			

General Words

Mastering the meanings of the words included in this section will contribute to your ability to comprehend material written on a college level. They are words that frequently appear in textbooks, newspapers, and periodicals like *Time*, *Newsweek*, and *Psychology Today*.

TYPES OF CONTEXTUAL CLUES

You will be given an opportunity to learn these words through the use of contextual clues, that is, by studying the relationship between an unfamiliar word and the other words surrounding it. Types of contextual clues that you will find particularly helpful in revealing an unknown word's meaning include the following:

■ **Direct Definition**

Have you even seen anyone wear a *monocle*, which is an eyeglass for just one eye?

Intrinsic motivation is a desire for action that comes from within an individual.

(Both sentences provide straightforward definitions of the italicized words.)

■ **Indirect Definition**

Although the pain was not intense, it was *chronic*, having been noticeable for the past two months.

Her desire for financial security was not a sufficient *rationale* for accepting his proposal.

(In the first sentence, "for the past two months" indicates that *chronic* describes something that lasts a long time; in the second sentence, "not a sufficient" suggests that *rationale* is a reason or a motive.)

■ **Examples**

Arthropods, such as crabs and lobsters, live in water.

Unrestricted television viewing can have *deleterious* effects on children, including apathy and insensitivity.

(In the first sentence, the examples of "such as crabs and lobsters" indicate that *arthropods* are animals that have a hard outer covering and jointed legs; in the second sentence, "apathy and insensitivity" suggest that *deleterious* describes something that is harmful.)

■ **Synonyms**

The *arbitrator*, or judge, ruled in favor of the club owners.

The president was *irate*; in other words, he was furious.

(In the first sentence, "or" makes it clear that *arbitrator* and *judge* are synonyms, that is, words with similar meanings. In the second sentence, "in other words" makes it obvious that *irate* and *furious* are synonyms.)

■ **Antonyms**

Early in her career, she was careless in her public remarks, but today she is much more *discreet*.

Although the mayor had been *churlish* lately, he was pleasant and agreeable at today's press conference.

(In the first sentence, "but" indicates that *careless* and *discreet* are antonyms, that is, words with opposite meanings. In the second sentence, "although" signifies that *churlish* has an opposite meaning to those of *pleasant and agreeable*.)

■ **Key Phrases Plus Knowledge of Word Parts**

The tyrant wanted to rule all of Europe; his attempt to *subjugate* the continent resulted in tragedy for thousands of people.

(The phrase "wanted to rule Europe," when combined with the knowledge that *sub-* means "under," provides the clue for understanding *subjugate*, which means "to put under authority.")

Infidelity is the only grounds for divorce in that country.

(The phrase "only grounds for divorce," when combined with the knowledge that *in-* means "not" and *fid* means "faith," provides the clue for understanding that *infidelity* means "not faithful.")

Specific contextual clues like the ones in the preceding examples are not always present to help unlock the meaning of an unfamiliar word. When that is the case, a reasonable inference about the unknown word can often be made by concentrating on what is being said about the subject of the sentence and by identifying the word's part of speech. Here is an example to illustrate this approach:

Bereft of money, friends, and jobs, numerous immigrants struggled to survive in the new world.

(It is stated that *immigrants*, the subject of the sentence, "struggled to survive." *Bereft* is an adjective; the combination of this information suggests that *bereft* is describing immigrants who *lacked* money, friends, and jobs. *Bereft*, then, means a "lack of" or "deprived of.")

Limitations of Contextual Clues

Although using contextual clues is generally reliable and is the most practical way of unlocking the meanings of unfamiliar words, you will find that this approach has its limitations. Specifically, contextual clues:

■ often reveal vague rather than precise meanings;

■ usually reveal a single meaning whereas most words have several;

■ are often absent or too obscure to be helpful;

■ seldom provide certainty of definition.

It should be clear, then, that there are times when you should consult a dictionary, particularly when you need complete and precise meanings of words or when you lack contextual clues.

Directions for Doing the Lessons

1. Familiarize yourself with each word's pronunciation according to the following pronunciation guide:

- a space separates each syllable;

- the accented syllable is printed in capital letters;

- vowels with long sounds have a line over them;

- the schwa sound (uh) in unaccented syllables is represented by ə, which looks like an upside-down e.

Examples: esoteric (es ə TER ik)
           utopian (ū TŌ pē an)

Note: The given pronunciation for each word in the lessons is the most common one, but there may be other pronunciations that are acceptable.

2. Observe the part of speech of each word; this knowledge can often serve as a helpful contextual clue. (Appendix A presents a concise review of parts of speech.)

3. Note that in the first part of each lesson some words contain a syllable that has been underlined because it is a word part that you studied in Section One; use your knowledge of this part, along with the insight gained through contextual clues, to deepen your understanding of the word.

4. Read the two sentences provided to illustrate the meaning of each word, being alert to the types of contextual clues that have been discussed.

5. Compose a definition for the word in your mind.

6. Consult a dictionary if contextual clues are absent or inadequate for you to form a definition of the word. (Appendix B presents helpful information about using a dictionary.)

7. Have your work checked after completing the four exercises in each lesson.

8. Be prepared for a mastery test after every even-numbered lesson. (The test will also include the ten words presented in the preceding odd-numbered lesson.)

Nouns: people, places, things

1. **acquisition** (ak wi ZISH ən)

   a. Ben's newest *acquisition*, a ten-speed bike, took almost all his savings.

   b. Adam's *acquisition* of carpentry skills resulted from his two years' work with a house-building company.

2. **catharsis** (kə THAR sis)

   a. Attending the local college basketball game appears to be a *catharsis* for Elliott, an air traffic controller. He's much more relaxed after he gets home from a game than he is when he gets home from work.

   b. As a *catharsis* for her anger, Mitzi took a long, brisk walk.

3. **deprivation** (dep rə VĀ shən)

   a. Although Warren's income was almost cut in half after he changed jobs, he was much happier, and he didn't seem to suffer any *deprivation*.

   b. After Ross was dismissed from his job, he endured one *deprivation* after another, including the loss of his home and his car as well as the inability to afford health insurance for his family and himself.

4. **gamut** (GAM ət)

   a. Herb's physical complaints ran the *gamut*, from headaches to ingrown toenails.

   b. Donna was administered a battery of tests, interviewed by four people, and shown the plant's various departments. After being put through such a demanding *gamut*, it was no wonder that she was exhausted at the end of the day.

5. **impasse** (IM pas)

   a. Because the union leaders had reached an *impasse* with the management representatives, the workers voted to strike.

   b. The young couple's *impasse* was caused by a disagreement over where they would spend their vacation.

6. **kin** (KIN)

   a. The president never publicly speaks critically of any of his *kin*.
   b. Most of Kathryn's *kin* are engaged in the lobster business in Maine.

7. <u>pre</u>emp<u>tion</u> (prē EMP shən)

   a. Victor is convinced that Uncle Bob's *preemption* of grandmother's estate will not stand up in court.
   b. The puppy's *preemption* of the old dog's blanket led to a quick but painful lesson for him.

8. **qualm** (KWAM)

   a. When Theo and I joined the air force, I had some fears, but he never expressed a single *qualm*.
   b. Despite a *qualm* or two, Mai gave her speech in front of the large audience.

9. **rancor** (RAN kor)

   a. Although the players had done poorly, the coach's *rancor* toward them was inexcusable.
   b. According to the testimony given by a number of witnesses, the defendant's *rancor* toward the victim was well known.

10. **rationale** (rash ə NAL)

    a. Ms. Burnell eloquently expressed her *rationale* for running for governor.
    b. Ivan realized that his desire to become wealthy wasn't considered a very lofty *rationale* for entering law school.

EXERCISES FOR LESSON 11
Nouns: people, places, things

I. *Directions:* Match each definition with the word it defines.

_____	**1.** acquisition	**a.** hatred, resentment
_____	**2.** catharsis	**b.** whole range, complete sequence
_____	**3.** deprivation	**c.** cleansing, discharge of pent-up emotions
_____	**4.** gamut	**d.** the act of claiming something before others
_____	**5.** impasse	**e.** motive, statement of reasons
_____	**6.** kin	**f.** possession, something acquired
_____	**7.** preemption	**g.** deadlock
_____	**8.** qualm	**h.** hardship, lack of the usual comforts or necessities of life
_____	**9.** rancor	**i.** uneasiness, misgiving
_____	**10.** rationale	**j.** a person's relatives

II. *Directions:* In each space, write the appropriate word from those listed below.

acquisition	deprivation	impasse	preemption	rancor
catharsis	gamut	kin	qualm	rationale

1. Morris took charge at the emergency site even though other police officers outranked him; however, his _____ of authority was not resented because he handled the situation in a commendable manner.

2. Anton and the salesman reached an _____ when they couldn't agree on a trade-in price for Anton's old Pontiac.

3. Claire is extremely angry at her boss. Her _____ is due to the fact that her promised promotion failed to materialize.

4. A punching bag in his basement served as a _____ for Norman. Whenever he got angry or tense, he headed downstairs to flail away at the bag.

5. Robin's most recent _____ is an antique clock.

6. Sam did have a _____ or two about asking Joan for a date, but he finally worked up his courage and asked her to go out with him next Friday evening.

7. The topics featured on the television show *60 Minutes* run the _____ from interesting interviews of famous people to in-depth reports of major crimes.

8. Although he's played golf for six year, Woody's _____ for taking lessons this season is that he recognizes he's never overcome some fundamental flaws in his swing.

9. Andrea said that the one _____ she experienced as an only child was not having a brother or sister to play with.

10. Lahta apparently loves her _____ because she makes the 800-mile trip to visit them at least twice a year.

III. *Directions:* Write *Yes* in the space if the italicized word is used correctly, *No* if it is not.

_____ 1. Kim's mother, who is forty-eight years old, is currently completing her freshman year at college; her *acquisition* and conscientiousness are admired by her fellow students.

_____ 2. Suffering from arthritis, poor eyesight, and *catharsis*, the dog was tenderly cared for by the old woman.

_____ 3. On his trip out West, Jeff's car lost some *deprivation* going through the mountains.

_____ 4. Mark realized that the *gamut* had value, but he was shocked to learn just how valuable it was after having it appraised.

_____ 5. I was surprised to see such a large *impasse* hitched to Tony's small truck.

_____ 6. Many of Michelle's *kin* live in Canada.

_____ 7. After receiving the disappointing report for the third quarter of the year, the corporation chairperson declared a low *preemption* for all shareholders.

_____ 8. After the many storms of winter, spring brought peace and *qualm* to the snug mountain village.

_____ 9. Susan couldn't understand her dog's *rancor* toward her little sister; perhaps she had teased him when he was a puppy.

        10. Kirk and Margie's *rationale* for being married this month instead of next October as originally planned is that they've recently been given an opportunity to buy a house located near where they both work.

IV. *Directions:* After selecting your response, put the letter that is before it in the space provided.

    1. The *opposite* of **qualm** is
       a. indifference
       b. uneasiness
       c. assurance

    2. The *opposite* of **rancor** is
       a. hostility
       b. love
       c. jealous

    3. The *opposite* of **impasse** is
       a. blockade
       b. agreement
       c. detour

    4. A **catharsis** provides
       a. anxiety
       b. excitement
       c. relief

    5. A **preemption** is similar to a
       a. promotion
       b. takeover
       c. summary

    6. **Rationale** is associated with
       a. motives
       b. measurements
       c. mannerisms

    7. The lack of the following would indicate a basic **deprivation**:
       a. luxuries
       b. food
       c. debts

_____ 8. The following is most likely to be a personal **acquisition**:
   a. taxi
   b. camera
   c. bridge

_____ 9. The word **gamut** suggests
   a. sameness
   b. variety
   c. immensity

_____ 10. **Kin** are
   a. relatives
   b. associates
   c. enemies

Nouns: people, places, things

1. **affluence** (AF loo əns)

   a. Japan's thriving economy has enabled its citizens to enjoy an impressive level of *affluence*.

   b. Mr. Donaldston used his *affluence* in many worthwhile ways, such as donating generously to numerous charities.

2. **alienation** (ā lē ə NĀ shən)

   a. President Woodrow Wilson's fervent hope was that the League of Nations formed after World War I would help end the *alienation* that had traditionally existed among many of the European nations.

   b. After the Tongs became acquainted with more people in the community, their feelings of *alienation* began to vanish.

3. **dichotomy** (dī KOT ə mē)

   a. Some parents, unfortunately, believe that a *dichotomy* exists between love and discipline when it comes to dealing with their children; actually, however, love and discipline go together.

   b. Because some members of the family wanted to go camping while others wanted to visit the zoo, Mr. Bradley suggested to his wife that the *dichotomy* be settled by camping on Friday night and visiting the zoo on Saturday.

4. **empathy** (EM pə thē)

   a. My *empathy* for my young friend was genuine because I could easily recall how upset I had felt when my dog died during my childhood.

   b. Many fans find it difficult to feel *empathy* for the striking ballplayers, whose salaries are already so high.

5. **enigma** (ə NIG mə)

    a. An *enigma* exists over why Lee Harvey Oswald assassinated President John F. Kennedy. It is a mystery that will probably never be solved.

    b. It's an *enigma* to their friends why the couple broke up, as they seemed perfect for each other.

6. <u>enmity</u> (EN mə t ē)

    a. As a result of bitter arguments over financial matters, *enmity* had unfortunately developed between the business partners.

    b. During boot camp, many of the recruits felt nothing but *enmity* toward their sergeant.

7. **fiasco** (fē AS kō)

    a. The actors simply hadn't spent enough time rehearsing, so the performance was a *fiasco*.

    b. Warren's efforts to make peace among his feuding in-laws became a *fiasco* because they were soon arguing again.

8. **nemesis** (NEM ə sis)

    a. Troy's *nemesis* in tennis was Mark; he could defeat all his opponents except Mark.

    b. Stuttering was a painful *nemesis* with which Carla struggled throughout her childhood.

9. **quintessence** (kwin TES əns)

    a. As far as I am concerned, she is the *quintessence* of what a lawyer should be.

    b. The Millers' home, located on Pine Street, is the *quintessence* of the Cape Cod style.

10. <u>recrimination</u> (rē krim ə NA shən)

    a. Mature individuals do not seek *recrimination* against those with whom they disagree.

    b. Ms. Reynolds sought *recrimination* against the dishonest mechanic by reporting him to the Better Business Bureau.

EXERCISES FOR LESSON 12
Nouns: people, places, things

I. *Directions:* Match each definition with the word it defines.

_____ 1. affluence	a. hatred, antagonism
_____ 2. alienation	b. puzzle, mystery
_____ 3. dichotomy	c. a complete failure, a blunder
_____ 4. empathy	d. abundance of wealth
_____ 5. enigma	e. the perfect embodiment or example
_____ 6. enmity	f. identifying with the feelings of others
_____ 7. fiasco	g. revenge, retaliation
_____ 8. nemesis	h. division into two parts, a split
_____ 9. quintessence	i. separation due to hostility or mistrust
_____ 10. recrimination	j. that which a person cannot conquer, a foe whom a person cannot best

II. *Directions:* In each space, write the appropriate word from those listed below.

affluence	dichotomy	enigma	fiasco	quintessence
alienation	empathy	enmity	nemesis	recrimination

1. The Olsons' trip down the Allagash River was a _____ as it rained all the time, black flies and mosquitoes were out in full force, and they ripped a hole in the bottom of their canoe.

2. Their hatred for each other was obvious, but no one knew the cause of their _____.

3. Most people have _____ for those who want to work but can't find jobs.

4. The _____ that initially existed between the two neighbors resulted from their different cultural backgrounds, but their suspicions of one another gradually disappeared as they got to know each other over the years.

5. Jay's neighbors complained about his loud stereo. In _____, he reported their pet goat to the authorities.

6. Two of the majestic mansions, built by people of enormous _____, were destroyed by the fire.

7. A _____ exists among the board members as six of the members favor the proposed merger while the other six oppose it.

8. As far as I am concerned, the red rose is the _____ of flowers.

9. Films directed by Alfred Hitchcock always contain an _____ that viewers find challenging to unravel.

10. Reverend Becker's _____ when he first began preaching was nervousness, but he eventually overcame this problem.

III. *Directions:* Write *Yes* in the space if the italicized word is used correctly, *No* if it is not.

_____ 1. Lobbyists try to *affluence* members of Congress to vote a certain way on particular bills.

_____ 2. The *alienation* that existed in the dormitory among some of the students disappeared as the school year progressed.

_____ 3. The doctor assured the patient that the *dichotomy* machine would relieve the muscular soreness in his back.

_____ 4. Darwin was usually a conscientious student; but, during a short period of the spring semester, he fell victim to *empathy*, and his grades went down.

_____ 5. Jeri got so much pleasure from driving her dependable jeep that she decided to equip it with an *enigma*.

_____ 6. The metropolitan area had once been nothing but a barren *enmity* between the two mountain ranges.

_____ 7. My sister is learning a style of painting called *fiasco*, which is painting using brushes of various sizes and shapes.

_____ 8. My dog's *nemesis* is a tough old tomcat that terrorizes all the other animals in the neighborhood.

_____ 9. Jacob did not enjoy the city park as much as he had because the disturbing *quintessence* of the larger crowds
made it more difficult for him to find peace and quiet.

_____ 10. After the Civil War, the radical Republicans in Congress
sought *recrimination* against the South.

IV. *Directions:* After selecting your response, put the letter that is before it in
the space provided.

____ 1. The *opposite* of **nemesis** is
   a. ally
   b. enemy
   c. follower

____ 2. The *opposite* of **enmity** is
   a. hate
   b. love
   c. jealousy

____ 3. The *opposite* of **affluence** is
   a. poverty
   b. power
   c. proficiency

____ 4. **Recrimination** is similar to
   a. reinforcement
   b. retaliation
   c. renovation

____ 5. **Enigma** : puzzle ::
         (is to)   (as)
   a. night : day
         (is to)
   b. crying : weeping
         (is to)
   c. dessert : dinner
         (is to)

_____ 6. **Fiasco** : failure ::
    a. triumph : defeat
    b. contest : score
    c. blueprint : plan

_____ 7. **Quintessence** suggests the
    a. best
    b. usual
    c. worst

_____ 8. **Alienation** suggests
    a. integration
    b. segregation
    c. participation

_____ 9. **Empathy** suggests
    a. identification with
    b. nervousness about
    c. misunderstanding over

_____ 10. If there is a **dichotomy**, then you would *not* expect
    a. debate
    b. disagreement
    c. harmony

Nouns: people, places, things

1. **am<u>bi</u>valence** (am BIV ə ləns)

   a. Ed's *ambivalence* is a result of his not knowing whether to join the navy or the marines.

   b. Helen's *ambivalence* about becoming a member of the repertory theater is understandable. She is a talented actress and loves all types of drama; on the other hand, she has little free time because she is taking a demanding premedical course in college.

2. **cliché** (klē SHĀ)

   a. It is often tempting to resort to a *cliché* to state our thoughts rather than taking the time to think of original expressions.

   b. Millie effectively discouraged the customer's flirting by shouting the *cliché* "Buzz off!"

3. **lethargy** (LETH ər jē)

   a. I discovered that watching television all day leads to *lethargy*, not to vitality.

   b. Margot's *lethargy* today is a result of her staying up all night studying.

4. **melee** (MĀ lā)

   a. A *melee* started when some fans became impatient for the concert to begin. Four people were injured, and eight others were arrested.

   b. Old cowboy movies often contain a *melee*, usually occurring in a saloon, in which the good guys in white hats wipe out the bad guys in black hats by punching them over tables, chairs, and upstairs banisters.

5. **novice** (NOV is)

   a. Julie, a *novice* at skiing, was embarrassed as she repeatedly fell from the tow bar.

   b. Currently, Carlotta is still a *novice* on the clarinet, but she hopes to be playing well enough by summer to be a member of the community band.

6. **quagmire** (KWAG mīr)

   a. After the storm, our yard was a regular *quagmire*.
   b. The trucking firm encountered a *quagmire* of regulations, making further expansion virtually impossible.

7. **subsidy** (SUB si dē)

   a. Some representatives are advocating a federal *subsidy* to save the state's largest corporation from bankruptcy.
   b. The young doctor agreed to open an office in the rural community after the members of the town council agreed to provide her with a *subsidy* until her practice was firmly established.

8. **subterfuge** (SUB tər fūj)

   a. In the 1972 Watergate affair both President Nixon and his close advisers were guilty of *subterfuge*.
   b. Elmo had to resort to *subterfuge* and lies to surprise his parents with a family party on their anniversary.

9. **trepidation** (trep i DĀ shən)

   a. Rose approached her first flying lesson with *trepidation*, but afterward she was thrilled and couldn't wait until the next lesson.
   b. Most people have feelings of *trepidation* when they are told by a doctor that they must be hospitalized.

10. **vestige** (VES tij)

    a. The only *vestige* to indicate that this metropolitan area was once an agricultural center is the large dairy farm located in the northern part of the county.
    b. Despite the old man's obvious pain and weakness, his eyes still sparkled with humor, a *vestige* of his unconquerable spirit.

EXERCISES FOR LESSON 13
Nouns: people, places, things

I. *Directions:* Match each definition with the word it defines.

_____ **1.** ambivalence   **a.** sluggishness, dullness, drowsiness

_____ **2.** cliché   **b.** fear, terror, alarm

_____ **3.** lethargy   **c.** amateur, beginner

_____ **4.** melee   **d.** a dull, common saying

_____ **5.** novice   **e.** novice

_____ **6.** quagmire   **f.** a mark or visible evidence

_____ **7.** subsidy   **g.** secret evasion of rules, the hiding of something

_____ **8.** subterfuge   **h.** swamp, bog, a difficult situation from which to get free

_____ **9.** trepidation   **i.** uncertainty, conflicting feelings

_____ **10.** vestige   **j.** riot, brawl, turmoil

II. *Directions:* In each space, write the appropriate word from those listed below.

| ambivalence | lethargy | novice | subsidy | trepidation |
| cliché | melee | quagmire | subterfuge | vestige |

1. Guy sometimes felt as if he were trapped in a _____ because he had been unable to free himself from his repetitious and boring job.

2. Although the scene looked like an absolute _____ to most fans, all the drivers in the demolition derby knew exactly what they were doing.

3. With soothing words, the nurse attempted to ease the young patient's _____.

4. Unsure whether Ellen had enjoyed their previous date, Roger's _____ about asking her to his family's house was understandable.

5. Dennis, sprawled on the couch, knew he would have to overcome his _____ if he hoped to be in good enough physical condition to accompany Paul on a cross-country bike trip.

6. The young stockbroker had been dishonest with many of her clients; when her _____ was finally discovered, she was indicted for fraud.

7. Miranda says that if she hears that _____ again, "Don't count your chickens before they hatch," she's going to scream!

8. Considering how well Kareem now plays the guitar, it is hard to believe that just a few months ago he was a _____ on this instrument.

9. The detective carefully examined the scene of the crime, hoping to find some _____ of recent activity.

10. In a number of countries, railroads receive a government _____ to help meet expenses.

III. *Directions:* Write *Yes* in the space if the italicized word is used correctly, *No* if it is not.

_____ 1. The mechanic believes that the *ambivalence* of Don's car is because the front wheels need to be aligned.

_____ 2. My veterinarian told me to hold my tomcat in a *cliché* while she gave him a shot.

_____ 3. Gene and Ann said that the cabinet's *lethargy* is patterned after one they had seen in Bermuda during their winter vacation.

_____ 4. A wild *melee* took place among the neighborhood dogs until their owners came and took charge.

_____ 5. The golf scores were not outstanding because the tournament had been limited to *novice* players.

_____ 6. Residents on Grant Street become disturbed when there is a heavy rain because the street becomes a virtual *quagmire*.

_____ 7. Sam cheerfully said that she wanted to go with them, but deep in her *subsidy*, she really didn't.

_____ 8. The judge angrily declared a mistrial when he learned that some of the evidence presented against the defendant had been obtained through *subterfuge*.

_____ **9.** After the mammoth bridge was thoroughly inspected, the examiner pronounced it completely safe and stated that motorists could now cross the bridge in confident *trepidation*.

_____ **10.** As she drifted lazily in her rowboat, Tahnee believed the ocean's *vestige* to be at least sixteen feet.

IV. *Directions:* After selecting your response, put the letter that is before it in the space provided.

_____ **1.** The *opposite* of **ambivalence** is
   a. uncertainty
   b. assurance
   c. hesitation

_____ **2.** A **cliché** is *not* associated with
   a. originality
   b. repetition
   c. familiarity

_____ **3.** **Quagmire** is associated with
   a. inspiration
   b. satisfaction
   c. frustration

_____ **4.** **Subterfuge** suggests
   a. consistency
   b. dishonesty
   c. simplicity

_____ **5.** **Subsidy** suggests
   a. aid
   b. bankruptcy
   c. prosperity

_____ **6.** **Vestige** : *trace* ::
   a. beautiful : plain
   b. hot : desert
   c. overflow : flood

_____ 7. **Novice** : *professional* ::
   a. girl scout : boy scout
   b. little leaguer : major leaguer
   c. private : sergeant

_____ 8. **Lethargy** : *vitality* ::
   a. tan : brown
   b. blue : purple
   c. black : white

_____ 9. **Trepidation** : *emotion* ::
   a. robbery : crime
   b. hesitation : boldness
   c. misbehavior : misconduct

_____ 10. If there is a **melee**, then you would *not* expect
   a. confusion
   b. calmness
   c. fisticuffs

Nouns: people, places, things

1. <u>com</u>plicity (kəm PLIS i tē)

    a. Even though the evidence presented against him was circumstantial, Mr. Randolph never denied his *complicity* in the crime engineered by his business associates.

    b. Blake deserved to get the ticket for speeding, but Tracy's *complicity* in the traffic violation was obvious to the others because it had been Tracy who kept urging Blake to drive faster.

2. <u>in</u>fidelity (in fi DEL i tē)

    a. Benedict Arnold's treason during the Revolutionary War is the most shocking *infidelity* in United States history.

    b. Christopher suspected that *infidelity* on his sister's part had contributed to the breakup of her marriage.

3. innuendo (in ū EN dō)

    a. The senator's opponent, by stressing the senator's friendships with several prominent business executives, suggested by *innuendo* that the senator was a mere pawn of big business.

    b. The clerk didn't actually say so, but implied by *innuendo* that if I bought the expensive lawnmower, he would give me a sizeable discount on a snowblower next fall.

4. nostalgia (nə STAL jə)

    a. Occasionally, Elaine will hear a song that was popular during her high school years, and she will long for her old friends and the activities they used to do together; such *nostalgia* is fleeting, however, because she does enjoy her life at college.

    b. The widow was swept with feelings of *nostalgia* as she tenderly picked up her husband's favorite pipe from his old desk.

5. <u>pan</u>orama (pan ə RAM ə)

   a. The summit of the mountain offers a *panorama* of the ruggedly beautiful Oregon coast.
   b. The professor's three-hour lecture, including slides and reproductions of period clothing, was a *panorama* of medieval history.

6. <u>prec</u>edent (PRESS i dənt)

   a. Dr. Michaels, Jane's psychology teacher, would not let her do a slide project rather than a research paper because he didn't want to set a *precedent*.
   b. Albert believes that the *precedent* for playing the national anthem at sporting events began during World War II.

7. quandary (KWON də rē)

   a. Mel was in a *quandary* over whether to attend the state university or the small college in her hometown.
   b. The truck driver was in a *quandary* because if he attempted to move his truck, he could slide down a steep embankment; however, if he didn't move it, he might be hit by traffic coming around the curve.

8. quirk (KWURK)

   a. Jessica's *quirk* is that she can't stand to hear anyone whistling.
   b. My dog runs to the fireplace and begins barking whenever the phone rings, a *quirk* in his behavior that I have never been able to understand.

9. <u>transition</u> (tran ZISH ən)

   a. Grandfather and Grandmother have many hobbies and interests, so their *transition* into retirement has been accomplished without any difficulty.
   b. The smooth *transition* from one scene to another is one of the major advantages movies have over live stage productions.

10. <u>vertigo</u> (VUR tə gō)

    a. People who suffer from *vertigo* don't like heights.
    b. After standing around for hours in the shopping mall lobby, Cody had feelings of *vertigo*; but after he sat down for a few minutes, the spinning sensation went away.

EXERCISES FOR LESSON 14
Nouns: people, places, things

I. *Directions:* Match each definition with the word it defines.

_____ 1. complicity

_____ 2. infidelity

_____ 3. innuendo

_____ 4. nostalgia

_____ 5. panorama

_____ 6. precedent

_____ 7. quandary

_____ 8. quirk

_____ 9. transition

_____ 10. vertigo

a. a longing for things, experiences, or people belonging to the past

b. a case that serves as a justification for similar cases, that which establishes a tradition

c. being an accomplice, involvement in wrongdoing

d. a state of uncertainty or doubt

e. an unobstructed, wide view

f. hint, sly suggestion, an indirect remark

g. movement from one position, stage, or condition to another

h. dizziness, a turning or whirling sensation

i. disloyalty, unfaithfulness, adultery

j. peculiarity, odd behavior

II. *Directions:* In each space, write the appropriate word from those listed below.

complicity	innuendo	panorama	quandary	transition
infidelity	nostalgia	precedent	quirk	vertigo

1. The campus newspaper reported recently that a few students have had their hair cut in the old-fashioned crewcut style because of _____ for the 1950s.

2. Ethel was in a _____. She found the apartment of her dreams; but, unless she could come up with the first month's rent in advance, she would not be able to take it.

3. How can we defend ourselves against anonymous accusations, rumor, and _____?

4. Leaving home for the first time is a major _____ in most people's lives.

5. Fritz's _____ in the practical joke that backfired was soon discovered.

6. After running up the eight flights of steps, Hannah suffered from _____, so she leaned against the wall until her head cleared.

7. Martha's car has a _____; when she turns sharply to the right, the horn beeps.

8. The article states that the television actress has quietly filed for divorce after hearing of her husband's _____.

9. Elvis Presley set the _____ for rock performance style in the late 1950s.

10. The Wongs are cutting down the trees on the edge of their property in order to have a _____ of the city skyline.

III. *Directions:* Write *Yes* in the space if the italicized word is used correctly, *No* if it is not.

_____ 1. Shelly loves engineering problems that involve *complicity* and challenge.

_____ 2. After the doctor heard an *infidelity* when Larry breathed deeply, she gave him a prescription for penicillin.

_____ 3. Fortunately, the new highway takes a wide *innuendo* around the congested metropolitan area.

_____ 4. Whenever my dad plays his Glenn Miller and Bing Crosby records, I know he has feelings of *nostalgia.*

_____ 5. Fortunately, the crowd did not break into a *panorama* when the fire was discovered.

_____ 6. Dr. Kenneth Cooper, who popularized jogging through his book *Aerobics,* established the *precedent* of using a point system for determining physical fitness levels.

_____ 7. Keller's *quandary* is that although his job pays extremely well, he does not like the work.

_____ 8. Jeff's *quirk* is shrugging his left shoulder every few seconds when he talks on the telephone.

_____ **9.** Wheat is the main *transition* of Canada's central provinces.

_____ **10.** Yesterday Mindy bought a new blue and *vertigo* blouse.

IV. *Directions:* After selecting your response, put the letter that is before it in the space provided.

____ **1. Transition** suggests
 a. assistance
 b. change
 c. promotion

____ **2. Innuendo** suggests
 a. foolishness
 b. kindliness
 c. slyness

____ **3. Complicity** suggests
 a. association
 b. negotiation
 c. opposition

____ **4. Panorama** suggests
 a. speed
 b. disorder
 c. scenery

____ **5. Quirk** : usual ::
 a. ordinary : routine
 b. interesting : boring
 c. familiar : customary

____ **6. Infidelity** : faithfulness ::
 a. courage : bravery
 b. generosity : charity
 c. unreliable : dependable

____ **7. Precedent** : model ::
 a. leader : follower
 b. law : jury
 c. pattern : example

_____ 8. **Nostalgia** : reunion ::
   a. sorrow : funeral
   b. joy : separation
   c. fatigue : exhaustion

_____ 9. You would most likely experience **vertigo** from
   a. talking to someone you disliked
   b. riding on a rollercoaster
   c. exercising daily

_____ 10. **Quandary** is *not* associated with
   a. assurance
   b. doubt
   c. frustration

Nouns: people, places, things

1. **apathy** (AP ə thē)

   a. A teacher who delights in what she teaches is deeply disappointed when students display *apathy* for the subject.

   b. I thought Mary would be eager to talk about her vacation, but she showed complete *apathy* when I asked her to tell me about it.

2. **compliance** (kəm PLĪ əns)

   a. Because the restaurant was not in *compliance* with the state's fire code, it was closed while the necessary changes were made.

   b. The judge's decision was that the defendant was in *compliance* with the terms of the contract.

3. **debacle** (dā BA kəl)

   a. Gordon's class reunion turned out to be a *debacle* because someone had failed to mail all the invitations, the restaurant manager had reserved the banquet for the wrong date, and the band didn't know any of the popular songs of the class's graduating year.

   b. Jacques threw his arms up in the air and laughingly complained that his grand plans for redecorating his apartment were quickly turning into a *debacle*. The wallpaper started coming off after he painted over it; then, the carpet store sent over a ghastly purple rug instead of the pale blue one he had ordered.

4. **decorum** (di KŌR əm)

   a. Although Mario lost the contest, his display of *decorum* both during and after the match earned him the respect of the fans.

   b. Amanda's sense of *decorum* kept her from reacting to the customer's rude behavior.

5. ela**tion** (i LA shən)

   a. The wildest *elation* I've ever seen was when our high school basketball team won the state championship.
   b. After they learned that the family would be going on a camping trip, the children expressed their *elation* by jumping up and down while squealing in delight.

6. **entourage** (ən too RAZH)

   a. Famous people always seem to have an *entourage*, which generally includes at least a secretary and a public relations person, traveling with them.
   b. Evelyn wanted to speak to Eric alone, but he was always part of the *entourage* that accompanied the boss on his trips.

7. **epitome** (i PIT ə mē)

   a. For many movie fans, Humphrey Bogart is the *epitome* of the rugged, romantic male hero.
   b. My literature teacher, who has admired the poetry of Robert Frost since her own college days, believes that Frost is the *epitome* of the American poet.

8. **idiosyncrasy** (id ē ə SIN krə sē)

   a. Ross's one *idiosyncrasy* is his refusal to answer the telephone after seven o'clock in the evening.
   b. An *idiosyncrasy* of my father's is his insistence that his cup of coffee contain a drop of vinegar.

9. **impunity** (im PŪ ni tē)

   a. Because he was a good friend of the local police chief, Matt thought he could ignore with *impunity* the town's posted speed limits. He quickly learned differently when he was slapped with a $75 fine for speeding.
   b. To his regret, the boxing champion discovered that he could not break training rules with *impunity* and still retain his championship against his well-conditioned opponent.

10. **re**gression (ri GRESH ən)

   a. Bernice is a mature, responsible person, but she acts like a twelve-year-old at parties. This kind of *regression* by adults, however, is common at such events.
   b. The experimenter was puzzled by the ape's *regression* to its former behavior of ignoring the bell instead of opening the door as it had been trained to do when the bell rang.

EXERCISES FOR LESSON 15
Nouns: people, places, things

I. *Directions:* Match each definition with the word it defines.

_____	**1.** apathy	**a.** great joy, high spirits
_____	**2.** compliance	**b.** the act of going back or returning, especially to a lesser or more primitive state
_____	**3.** debacle	**c.** peculiarity, oddness
_____	**4.** decorum	**d.** freedom from punishment, exemption from detrimental effects
_____	**5.** elation	**e.** indifference, absence of emotion, lack of interest
_____	**6.** entourage	**f.** politeness, behavior characterized by dignity
_____	**7.** epitome	**g.** a person or thing that possesses the perfect example of the features of a whole class of people or things
_____	**8.** idiosyncrasy	**h.** the act of conforming, cooperating, or obeying
_____	**9.** impunity	**i.** a group of personal attendants and followers
_____	**10.** regression	**j.** a complete failure, a great disaster

II. *Directions:* In each space, write the appropriate word from those listed below.

apathy	debacle	elation	epitome	impunity
compliance	decorum	entourage	idiosyncrasy	regression

1. The double date turned into a _____ because one of the couples got into a pouting mood that lasted all evening.

2. The wealthy basketball player possessed the _____ of a luxurious automobile—a Rolls Royce.

3. Instead of improving, the children's behavior showed clear signs of _____ after they spent a month with their grandparents.

4. Kindergarten helps children to learn that they must consider the effects of their acts on others, that they cannot misbehave with _____.

5. After extensive renovations, the majestic old inn was now in _____ with the state's new safety code.

6. Even though exhausted, Tom felt great _____ after he finally reached the mountain's summit.

7. I observed Luke's _____ when Hedwig went on and on about the super modifications she had made in her car's engine. Luke, I knew, had never been interested in the mechanical aspects of cars.

8. Dawn lost her usual _____ when it was announced at the assembly that she had been selected to attend West Point.

9. Nancy feels that everyone is entitled to at least one _____, and hers is collecting old restaurant menus.

10. The actress's _____ included a press agent, a hairdresser, and a secretary.

III. *Directions:* Write *Yes* in the space if the italicized word is used correctly, *No* if it is not.

_____ 1. The grounds of the estate were covered with flowers, *apathy*, shrubs, and fountains.

_____ 2. The police warned that anyone not in *compliance* with the new public drinking law would be arrested on the spot.

_____ 3. Frustrated because he could not loosen the bolts from the wheel, Davis angrily threw the *debacle* jack into the ditch alongside the road.

_____ 4. The gymnasium was hardly recognizable after the committee placed *decorum* throughout its length and width.

_____ 5. The paramedics exercised supreme *elation* as they attempted to remove the injured woman from the car.

_____ 6. The corporation president's *entourage* was reduced somewhat when the board of directors refused to pay for his chauffeur and his private physician.

_____ 7. In the *epitome* of the business section was a small park containing a statue honoring residents who had served in the armed forces.

_____ 8. Raoul bought the *idiosyncrasy* from his neighbor even though he thought the price was a little steep.

_____ 9. The owners of the cottages around the lake were upset when they learned of the lake's *impunity*.

_____ 10. Nadine started as a cashier, but due to her rapid *regression*, she was soon promoted to the loan department.

IV. *Directions:* After selecting your response, put the letter that is before it in the space provided.

_____ 1. The *opposite* of **regression** is
   a. suspicion
   b. progression
   c. concentration

_____ 2. The *opposite* of **compliance** is
   a. defiance
   b. submission
   c. nonresistance

_____ 3. The *opposite* of **apathy** is
   a. indifference
   b. coldness
   c. passion

_____ 4. **Impunity** suggests
   a. panic
   b. privilege
   c. punishment

_____ 5. **Epitome** is associated with
   a. equality
   b. inferiority
   c. superiority

_____ 6. **Entourage** : followers ::
   a. class : students
   b. team : fans
   c. congregation : ministers

_____ 7. **Idiosyncrasy** : wearing polka dot shoes ::
   a. peculiarity : shopping for groceries
   b. hobby : collecting stamps
   c. eccentricity : entertaining guests

_____ 8. **Elation** : emotion ::
   a. red : color
   b. joy : happiness
   c. questions : understanding

_____ 9. **Decorum** : behavior ::
   a. manners : conduct
   b. points : scoring
   c. disturbance : tranquility

_____ 10. If a **debacle** occurs, then you would expect
   a. jubilation
   b. starvation
   c. chaos

Nouns: people, places, things

1. **alias** (Ā lē əs)

    a. Jim Rockford, a private investigator, often used an *alias* rather than his own name to obtain information from unsuspecting people.

    b. Why in the world does Wesley sometimes use the *alias* "David Snow" when he answers the department's telephone?

2. **bliss** (BLIS)

    a. A challenging job, an attractive apartment, good friends, and improved health brought *bliss* to Marie-Laure's life.

    b. When the radio announcer said that school was canceled for the day because of the snowstorm, Mike had a feeling of *bliss* come over him as he went back to sleep.

3. **cessation** (se SĀ shən)

    a. The college's outreach program continued to operate and to thrive even though the *cessation* of federal funds had occurred two years before.

    b. The *cessation* of the long rainy season meant that the farmers could finally plant their crops.

4. **consternation** (kon stər NĀ shən)

    a. Because his patient's condition was so serious, Dr. Johnson's *consternation* about his inability to diagnose the cause of the illness was understandable.

    b. John displayed considerable *consternation* when his check didn't come in the mail; his landlord had threatened to evict him if he didn't receive payment immediately.

5. **contemporary** (kən TEM pə rer ē)

    a. As did his *contemporary*, J.R.R. Tolkien, C.S. Lewis taught English at Oxford University and wrote fantasy novels.

    b. In the summer, Shelby, a childhood *contemporary*, and I would often ride over to Karle's Bakery to buy doughnuts after we had been swimming.

6. **duress** (doo RES)

   a. Even under *duress*, the little boy refused to disclose why he had skipped school that day.
   b. No one chooses to live under the *duress* of dictatorship.

7. **euphemism** (Ū fə miz əm)

   a. "Senior citizen" is a *euphemism* for "old person."
   b. Usually in ad campaigns the words "false teeth" are not used; instead, the *euphemism* "dentures" is heard.

8. **guise** (GĪZ)

   a. Using the *guise* of a photographer, Marco gained entrance to the church to witness the wedding of the two rock stars.
   b. The policeman, dressed in the *guise* of an old woman, strolled slowly in the neighborhood where muggers had frequently attacked.

9. **hypocrite** (HIP ə krit)

   a. After scolding his roommate for not studying more, Koto felt like a *hypocrite* when he decided to go to the hockey game rather than to the library to study.
   b. Coach Bouchard is certainly not a *hypocrite* when she stresses that everyone should attempt to stay in good physical condition; she's an active hiker, swimmer, and handball player.

10. **incumbent** (in KUM bənt)

    a. Marilyn Rayne, the *incumbent*, defeated her challenger for the post of district representative in the state legislature.
    b. Rumors are circulating that Gretchen will become the television station's director of advertising when the *incumbent* in that position retires next year.

EXERCISES FOR LESSON 16
Nouns: people, places, things

I. *Directions:* Match each definition with the word it defines.

_____ 1. alias   a. a mild or vague word used in place of one thought to be offensive or disagreeable

_____ 2. bliss   b. living or occurring at the same time

_____ 3. cessation   c. a person who pretends to have qualities or virtues he or she does not possess

_____ 4. consternation   d. supreme happiness

_____ 5. contemporary   e. an assumed name

_____ 6. duress   f. external appearance, assumed likeness

_____ 7. euphemism   g. bewilderment or dismay that causes confusion

_____ 8. guise   h. the ending or stopping, termination

_____ 9. hypocrite   i. the occupant or holder of an office or position

_____ 10. incumbent   j. pressure exerted in an effort to compel a person to some action or statement, compulsion by threat

II. *Directions:* In each space, write the appropriate word from those listed below.

alias	cessation	contemporary	euphemism	hypocrite
bliss	consternation	duress	guise	incumbent

  1. Unlike many famous entertainers who change their names, Bruce Springsteen has never used an _____.

2. The suspect testified in court that his confession to the police had been made under _____.

3. Patricia McKnight was elected to the local school board, defeating the _____ by a substantial margin.

4. Thierry's _____ is due to his fiancée's delay in setting a wedding date.

5. When Alison replied "different" after he had asked her how he looked in his new hairstyle, Pierre knew she had just used a _____ for "lousy."

6. _____ for Alan was a warm summer day with nothing to do but tinker with his 1957 Chevrolet.

7. I felt like a _____ after criticizing my daughter for driving too fast, for I realize that I'm often guilty of the same thing.

8. The retired politician had been a _____ of President Eisenhower.

9. Wells often dressed in the _____ of a jogger, but no one ever saw him run.

10. The retirement of Mr. and Mrs. Dabler last month meant the _____ of a family business that had prospered in the community for thirty-seven years.

III. *Directions:* Write *Yes* in the space if the italicized word is used correctly, *No* if it is not.

_____ **1.** John Topping, a popular disk jockey in Missouri, uses the *alias* "Johnny Spin" on the air.

_____ **2.** Except for the *bliss*, which needed to be repainted, the boat was in good shape.

_____ **3.** The *cessation* of "Rodeo Days" brought tranquility back to the community.

_____ **4.** Wendy had been leading the race until she sprained her ankle, so her *consternation* is understandable.

_____ **5.** Gene Autry and Roy Rogers were *contemporary* heroes in Western movies.

_____ **6.** Despite the feelings of *duress* most members mentioned, the company's board of directors refused to make an immediate decision as to whether or not to accept the merger offer.

_____ **7.** The soothing *euphemism* of the music played in the background of the department store.

_____ **8.** Crystal loved living in the Southwest although at times she missed Oregon's *guise* of trees and mountains.

_____ **9.** Maury sometimes suffers from a *hypocrite* shoulder caused by an old football injury.

_____ **10.** They decided to place the tiny baby boy into an *incumbent* until he grew stronger.

IV. *Directions:* After selecting your response, put the letter that is before it in the space provided.

____ **1.** A **contemporary** would most likely share your
    a. preferences
    b. friends
    c. culture

____ **2.** **Consternation** is *not* associated with
    a. confusion
    b. calm
    c. frustration

____ **3.** **Hypocrite** : pretense ::
    a. adherent : deception
    b. believer : sincerity
    c. critic : praise

____ **4.** **Alias** : toupee ::
    a. assumed name : wig
    b. pen name : actor
    c. clever deception : trickery

____ **5.** **Guise** : deceive ::
    a. disintegrate : dissolve
    b. dishonor : tribute
    c. counterfeit : fool

____ **6.** **Euphemism** : bluntness
    a. alibi : excuse
    b. height : altitude
    c. smooth : rough

_____ 7. **Duress** suggests
   a. cooperation
   b. free will
   c. force

_____ 8. The *opposite* of **bliss** is
   a. delight
   b. interest
   c. misery

_____ 9. The *opposite* of **incumbent** is
   a. challenger
   b. client
   c. candidate

_____ 10. The *opposite* of **cessation** is
   a. intermission
   b. genesis
   c. termination

Nouns: people, places, things

1. <u>col</u>lateral (kə LAT ər əl)

   a. To obtain financing for their purchase of the motel, the Eddicotts used their lumber business as *collateral.*
   b. Milo plans to use his pickup truck as *collateral* to secure a bank loan.

2. <u>con</u>jecture (kən JEK chər)

   a. It is only *conjecture,* but Joe believes the reason his sister and her husband moved to another state was because they were tired of their relatives dropping in on them all the time.
   b. Naturally, there is plenty of *conjecture* as to why the Bells are getting a divorce, but no one knows for sure.

3. <u>cre</u>dence (KRĒD əns)

   a. The discovery of such artifacts as primitive tools, weapons, and pottery adds *credence* to the long-held belief that the small New Mexico town was once the home of a prehistoric people.
   b. The sportswriter asked the athletic director if he could provide *credence* to the rumor that the basketball coach had been asked to resign.

4. <u>de</u>terrent (di TUR ənt)

   a. Using apples and gum as a *deterrent,* Vicki successfully kicked her smoking habit.
   b. Farmers use scarecrows in the garden to serve as a *deterrent* to birds.

5. <u>dex</u>terity (dek STER i tē)

   a. Lili's *dexterity* in driving the truck with a 42-foot trailer was demonstrated when she expertly backed down a narrow alley.
   b. Dentistry requires a high degree of manual *dexterity.*

6. **farce** (FARS)

   a. The movie, which was advertised as another *Gone with the Wind*, turned out to be a *farce*; the characters were particularly absurd.
   b. Vincent's tape recording was a *farce* because he was much too far away from the stage; his recording sounded as if some gerbils were squealing and dancing on a tin roof during a hailstorm.

7. **hypochondriac** (hī pə KON drē ak)

   a. It is well known that Mr. Salandi is a *hypochondriac*, worrying that every little ailment afflicting him is the forerunner of a major illness.
   b. Kathy believes that Vance is a *hypochondriac*, so she didn't get too upset when he started to complain about a backache.

8. **interim** (IN tər im)

   a. In the *interim* between graduating from high school and joining the marines, Rico worked in a plastics factory.
   b. Lenore told me that she eventually wants to have a restaurant of her own, but that in the *interim* she would accept the job as the inn's major chef.

9. **labyrinth** (LAB ə rinth)

   a. Trying to follow the directions to the interstate highway was like trying to find an escape from a *labyrinth*.
   b. Because the winter and spring storms had washed away many of the path's rocks and wooden markers, the winding trail around the mountain was an extremely difficult *labyrinth* to figure out.

10. **liaison** (lē ā ZON)

    a. The president chose a former senator to act as *liaison* between the executive and congressional branches of government.
    b. Mr. Costano, who speaks a number of languages fluently, is the *liaison* between the recently arrived foreign students and their faculty advisers.

EXERCISES FOR LESSON 17
Nouns: people, places, things

I. *Directions:* Match each definition to the word part it defines.

_____ **1.** collateral   **a.** something that discourages or prevents

_____ **2.** conjecture   **b.** security pledged for the payment of a loan

_____ **3.** credence   **c.** one who imagines that he or she is in ill health

_____ **4.** deterrent   **d.** coordinator, communicator between two groups

_____ **5.** dexterity   **e.** a guess, an opinion formed without sufficient evidence for proof

_____ **6.** farce   **f.** riddle, complex path, maze, anything that is bewildering by its complexity

_____ **7.** hypochondriac   **g.** manual efficiency, nimbleness, physical skill

_____ **8.** interim   **h.** an intervening period of time, interval

_____ **9.** labyrinth   **i.** belief, that which supports as true

_____ **10.** liaison   **j.** a ridiculous performance, a foolish imitation

II. *Directions:* Selecting from the list below, write the proper word part in each spaces so that the appropriate word is formed.

collateral	credence	dexterity	hypochondriac	labyrinth
conjecture	deterrent	farce	interim	liaison

1. Many people do not feel that capital punishment is an effective _____ against serious crimes.

2. The doctor, who worried about every little pain she got, was a worse _____ than any of her patients.

3. Deedee used her vast real estate holdings as _____ for a loan to expand her florist business.

4. The "gigantic" circus was a _____ as there were only three rides and a half-dozen amusements.

5. Because of her _____ on the drums, Farrah is often asked to play in bands, ranging from those that play rock to those that play symphonies.

6. Students sometimes feel that the university library, because of its huge size and numerous specialized areas, is a _____ that they will never master.

7. _____ at the plant was that Walter would be the one promoted to the supervisory position.

8. During the _____ between his high school graduation and his college years, Donald worked in Quebec.

9. Mr. Burns agreed to serve as the company's _____ overseas after being offered a substantial raise.

10. The discovery of an old Bible with the words "Edinburgh, Scotland" written on the inside flyleaf lent _____ to Gilbert's assertion that his mother's ancestors had come from Scotland.

III. *Directions:* Write *Yes* in the space if the italicized word is used correctly, *No* if it is not.

_____ 1. The Russos have such good credit at the bank that it is unnecessary for them to provide *collateral* for small loans.

_____ 2. For the informal meeting, Debbie arranged the tables and chairs in a *conjecture*.

_____ 3. The doctor provided *credence* to the plaintiff's claim that his recent disability was directly related to an automobile accident he was involved in two years ago.

_____ 4. The chairperson did an effective job of conducting the meeting as she would allow only those subjects listed on the *deterrent* to be discussed.

_____ 5. Roland's *dexterity* with car tools is admired by his friends.

_____ 6. Janice insisted that the apartment have a *farce* so that she would have room for a washer and dryer.

_____ 7. Grandfather had been a *hypochondriac* all of his life, so no one in the family was concerned when he started complaining of stomach pains.

_____ **8.** The map clearly showed that an *interim* lake was located in the southern part of the country.

_____ **9.** Jackson went into an absolute *labyrinth* after mowing his large yard on a hot, humid day.

_____ **10.** The trustees suggested that a qualified person be hired to serve as a *liaison* between the college and the alumni living on the West Coast.

IV. *Directions:* After selecting your response, put the letter that is before it in the space provided.

_____ **1.** A **hypochondriac** is likely to
   a. inspire
   b. exaggerate
   c. supervise

_____ **2.** The *opposite* of **dexterity** is
   a. agility
   b. brutality
   c. clumsiness

_____ **3.** **Liaison** suggests
   a. coordination
   b. inefficiency
   c. hardship

_____ **4.** The word closest in meaning to **interim** is
   a. maturity
   b. pause
   c. interference

_____ **5.** A **deterrent** does *not*
   a. discontinue
   b. limit
   c. encourage

_____ **6.** **credence** : support ::
   a. embrace : repel
   b. discredit : injure
   c. question : answer

_____ 7. **farce** : ridicule ::
    a. normal : odd
    b. business : profit
    c. success : praise

_____ 8. **conjecture** : fact ::
    a. suggestion : advice
    b. theory : certainty
    c. presume : guess

_____ 9. **collateral** : pledge ::
    a. oath : vow
    b. harmony : controversy
    c. testimony : truth

_____ 10. A **labyrinth** is *not* associated with
    a. fatigue
    b. simpleness
    c. bewilderment

Nouns: people, places, things

1. <u>correlation</u> (kor ə LĀ shən)

   a. Our college conducted a study that found a positive *correlation* between the students' grades and their extracurricular activities.
   b. My math teacher said that there is a *correlation* between mathematics skills and computer ability, but that this relationship isn't as strong as we might think.

2. <u>fidelity</u> (fi DEL i tē)

   a. Most presidents of the United States have demonstrated a *fidelity* to the spirit as well as to the principles of the Constitution.
   b. Paula's *fidelity* to the exercises prescribed by the doctor enabled her to recover quickly from her knee surgery.

3. <u>iconoclast</u> (ī KON ə klast)

   a. Frances is such an *iconoclast*; she is opposed to marriage, religion, sports—even apple pie!
   b. My parents consider me an *iconoclast* because I am opposed to family reunions and anniversary celebrations.

4. <u>myriad</u> (MIR ē əd)

   a. Lately, Carlos has had a *myriad* of problems with his car: the brakes failed, the exhaust system leaked, and the battery died.
   b. Take along this insect repellent when you go fishing because there is certain to be a *myriad* of bugs.

5. <u>pariah</u> (pə RĪ ə)

   a. Stefanie was treated like a *pariah* by the people in the small community because she had lived there for only four years.
   b. Michael, who didn't care for sports, was treated like a *pariah* by the jocks in the dorm.

6. **parley** (PAR lē)

   a. After a long *parley*, the college's trustees were still undecided whether or not to approve a program in x-ray technology.

   b. Shari's parents said that there would be a family *parley* after dinner to discuss a job offer her father had received from a firm in another state.

7. **prognosis** (prog NŌ sis)

   a. Despite the fact that Coach Bradshaw suffered a serious heart attack, the *prognosis* for his recovery is very good.

   b. Ms. Katzen's *prognosis* is that computers will be as common as television sets in most American homes by the end of this decade.

8. **provocation** (prov ə KĀ shən)

   a. As a result of the child's persistent *provocation*, the puppy bit him on the arm.

   b. The store manager warned all employees that taking any merchandise without paying for it would be adequate *provocation* for being fired.

9. **retrospect** (RE trə spekt)

   a. Mr. Hanson said that, in *retrospect*, one of the happiest periods of his life was the four years he spent in the navy.

   b. In *retrospect*, Neal was sorry that he had become sarcastic with the automobile dealer over the minor problems he had with his new car.

10. **solace** (SOL is)

   a. Doreen often sought *solace* for her loneliness by taking long walks through the city's streets.

   b. It doesn't take a genius to realize that it is a bad mistake to seek *solace* from troubles in drinking.

EXERCISES FOR LESSON 18
Nouns: people, places, things

I. *Directions:* Match each definition to the word part it defines.

_____ **1.** correlation   **a.** discussion, conference, meeting

_____ **2.** fidelity   **b.** a mutual relation of two or more things, an orderly connection

_____ **3.** iconoclast   **c.** comfort, reassurance, relief from affliction

_____ **4.** myriad   **d.** an outcast, a person generally despised and avoided

_____ **5.** pariah   **e.** something that angers, irritates, or incites

_____ **6.** parley   **f.** loyalty, faithfulness, accuracy, or exactness

_____ **7.** prognosis   **g.** countless, a very great number

_____ **8.** provocation   **h.** a look back, hindsight, a reference to previous times

_____ **9.** retrospect   **i.** attacker of cherished or traditional beliefs

_____ **10.** solace   **j.** forecast, prediction, the prospect of recovery

II. *Directions:* Selecting from the list below, write the proper word part in each space so that the appropriate word is formed.

correlation	iconoclast	pariah	prognosis	retrospect
fidelity	myriad	parley	provocation	solace

1. In _____, Randy wished he hadn't loaned his Datsun because it was now two hours past the time his roommate said he would return the car.

2. The members of the trailer caravan scheduled a _____ when they reached a state park in western Colorado to organize their sightseeing agenda.

General Words Lesson 18   111

3. ReAnne felt like a _____ at the party because she saw no one she knew, and no one bothered to talk to her.

4. Vikram, who is a navigator in the air force, says that there is a strong _____ between mathematical skills and navigational skills.

5. The sweltering heat and the heavy traffic congestion provided ample _____ for losing one's patience, but Nora remained serene.

6. Ms. West's _____ to the company was recognized when she was given a large bonus at Christmastime.

7. Ray appreciated the _____ his friends provided after his divorce.

8. Heidi and Shirley delighted in telling their friends about their _____ activities, which range from scuba diving to mountain climbing.

9. The doctor's _____ was that Barney would make a complete recovery from his serious injuries.

10. Mention any social institutions and Sharon will be sure to say negative things about them; I've never known such an _____.

III. *Directions:* Write *Yes* in the space if the italicized word is used correctly, *No* if it is not.

_____ 1. The rodeo in Cheyenne brought a *correlation* crowd from all parts of the nation.

_____ 2. The salesperson pointed out the impressive color *fidelity* of the expensive television set.

_____ 3. The construction plans call for expensive *iconoclast* reinforcement for the exterior walls.

_____ 4. The reflection of the *myriad* indicated that the infection was gone.

_____ 5. The impressive-looking man had once been elected *pariah* of the island, and he had governed in a progressive manner.

_____ 6. After the committee held a long *parley*, Ernie was selected to go to the club's national convention.

_____ 7. Throughout the winter months, Debra made steady *prognosis* playing the clarinet.

_____ 8. The judge disallowed the defendant's assertion that he struck the police officer only after extreme *provocation*.

9. The television special provided an interesting *retrospect* of America during World War II.

10. The *solace* of the occasion prevented Otis from discussing his plans with his family.

IV. *Directions:* After selecting your responses, put the letter that is before it in the space provided.

1. **Myriad** suggests
   a. many
   b. wealth
   c. complexity

2. The *opposite* of **fidelity** is
   a. reliability
   b. disloyalty
   c. correspondence

3. **Provocation** is certainly *not*
   a. gratifying
   b. infuriating
   c. exasperating

4. **Parley** : conference ::
   a. meeting : participants
   b. discussion : talk
   c. negotiation : treaty

5. **Solace** : admonish ::
   a. promptness : punctual
   b. comfort : aid
   c. reward : punishment

6. **Retrospect** : review ::
   a. reminiscence : recollection
   b. recollection : forgetfulness
   c. forgetfulness : memory

7. **Prognosis** : forecast ::
   a. fortuneteller : prophecy
   b. weather : rain
   c. prediction : foretelling

_____ 8. You would not expect a **pariah** to be
   a. popular
   b. rejected
   c. disowned

_____ 9. **Correlation** is concerned with
   a. relationship
   b. expansion
   c. forgiveness

_____ 10. Which one would most likely be an **iconoclast**?
   a. politician
   b. skeptic
   c. celebrity

Verbs: action words

1. **abhor** (ab HOR)

   a. I don't *abhor* tomato juice; I just like orange juice better, particularly for breakfast.
   b. Taylor does *abhor* smoking.

2. **abstain** (ab STĀN)

   a. Dr. Rodgers, my political science instructor, believes a person should *abstain* from voting if he or she hasn't studied the issues.
   b. My roommate said he would *abstain* from cracking his knuckles if I would stop snapping my gum.

3. **demean** (di MĒN)

   a. The president apparently feels that our country will *demean* itself if it responds in an aggressive manner to such verbal abuse.
   b. Don't *demean* yourself by accepting such a low salary.

4. **emanate** (EM ə nāt)

   a. During an international crisis, many confidential messages will generally *emanate* from the president's office.
   b. Compassion and concern seemed to *emanate* from the doctor's face.

5. **impede** (im PĒD)

   a. You will *impede* the recovery of your sprained ankle if you go jogging today.
   b. Eduardo wants to get more education and training because he doesn't want to *impede* his chances of reaching the top management levels of his company.

115

6. **rationalize** (RASH nə līz)

    a. Sometimes we *rationalize* our mistakes rather than take direct steps to correct them.

    b. Marie will sometimes *rationalize* her dog's misbehavior by saying that he's not naughty, just high-spirited.

7. **scrutinize** (SKROOT ə nīz)

    a. Be sure to *scrutinize* each section of that contract before signing your name.

    b. Ms. Phillips said that she will *scrutinize* carefully every application for the position before she makes a decision to hire.

8. **stipulate** (STIP yə lat)

    a. Among the requirements mentioned for the term paper, the professor did *stipulate* that it must be typed.

    b. Be sure to *stipulate* how you want your hair cut because that barber has a tendency to cut too much.

9. **vacillate** (VAS ə lāt)

    a. Charles did *vacillate* over whether or not to keep or to give up his throne; he finally decided to relinquish it.

    b. Although she realized that her boss did not appreciate her uncertainty, Natalie would *vacillate* every time she was asked whether she would accept a transfer to a plant in another state.

10. **yearn** (YURN)

    a. Jim Seventrees enjoyed skiing so much that even when the temperature went below zero, he did not *yearn* for the coziness of the lodge.

    b. Chuck enjoyed being in the navy, but sometimes he would *yearn* to see his old high school friends.

EXERCISES FOR LESSON 19
Verbs: action words

I. *Directions:* Match each definition to the word part it defines.

_____	**1.** abhor	**a.** to lower in dignity, to debase
_____	**2.** abstain	**b.** to have a strong desire for
_____	**3.** demean	**c.** indecisive, to waver in opinion
_____	**4.** emanate	**d.** to hate, to detest
_____	**5.** impede	**e.** to explain away, to justify
_____	**6.** rationalize	**f.** to not do something, to refrain
_____	**7.** scrutinize	**g.** to examine carefully
_____	**8.** stipulate	**h.** to send forth, to flow out
_____	**9.** vacillate	**i.** to make a specific demand, to require as an essential condition
_____	**10.** yearn	**j.** to hinder, to obstruct

II. *Directions:* In each space, write the appropriate word from those listed below.

abhor	demean	impede	scrutinize	vacillate
abstain	emanate	rationalize	stipulate	yearn

1. David said he would _____ the want ads every day until he found a job for which he was qualified.

2. The little boy hid from his mother because he was afraid that her scolding would _____ him in the sight of his two close friends.

3. Trudy did make numerous excuses for her disappointing grades last semester, but I don't think she will have to _____ her grades this semester; she's been studying long hours every day.

4. Charles said that he did _____ about whether to major in English or journalism, but he finally decided on the latter.

5. Brock said he would have to do better in chemistry this semester since another mediocre grade in this subject would _____ his chances of getting into medical school.

6. The new doctor told Tanya that she would be wise to _____ from smoking.

7. Heinz used to _____ the winter months, but since he learned to ski a couple of years ago, he can't wait for the first snowflake of the season to fall.

8. Gabrielle said the dentist did _____ that she should stop eating so many sweets if she wanted to avoid having any more cavities.

9. As evening approached, a cool, refreshing breeze began to _____ from across the lake.

10. Les still did _____ for a motorcycle even though he promised his wife when they got married that he would not buy one.

III. *Directions:* Write *Yes* in the space if the italicized word is used correctly, *No* if it is not.

_____ 1. I have a fondness for sweet potatoes, so I *abhor* them any time they are served.

_____ 2. Although it is not an ordinary discoloration, the *abstain* can be removed with paint remover.

_____ 3. Archie's tennis style is always aggressive and *demean*, since he is never content just to keep the ball in play.

_____ 4. The long run may *emanate* you, but, after a few minutes, you will feel on top of the world.

_____ 5. Lack of rain may *impede* this year's corn harvest.

_____ 6. When you go camping, it is particularly important to *rationalize* your food and other supplies so that if you do get lost, you will be able to survive.

_____ 7. Tightly *scrutinize* the bottle's cap so that vapors don't escape.

_____ 8. Heather advised us to *stipulate* our papers together so they would be easier to read.

_____ 9. Rory said I should *vacillate* my tires to get a smoother ride.

_____ 10. Do you ever *yearn* for a new car?

IV. *Directions:* After selecting your response, put the letter that is before it in the space provided.

_____ **1. Scrutinize** suggests someone being
    a. careful
    b. emotional
    c. reckless

_____ **2. Vacillate** suggests someone being
    a. powerful
    b. hesitant
    c. determined

_____ **3.** Which words are most closely associated with **emanate**?
    a. fight with
    b. gather in
    c. proceed from

_____ **4. Abstain** : participate ::
    a. humble : proud
    b. refuse : deny
    c. avoid : shun

_____ **5. Impede** : retard ::
    a. close : open
    b. hinder : help
    c. poor : needy

_____ **6. Yearn** : hope for ::
    a. desire : work for
    b. hanker : plan for
    c. covet : wish for

_____ **7. Abhor** : love ::
    a. loathe : hate
    b. despise : adore
    c. detest : scorn

_____ **8.** The *opposite* of **demean** is
    a. acclaim
    b. bargain
    c. compare

_____ **9.** Which word would you associate with **stipulate**?
   a. compatibility
   b. aimlessness
   c. demand

_____ **10.** If you **rationalize,** then you do *not*
   a. explain
   b. confess
   c. philosophize

Verbs: action words

1. **adulterate** (ə DUL tə rāt)

   a. The winegrower insisted that he would never *adulterate* his wine with water or chemicals.
   b. Laboratory studies revealed that the paint contained an insignificant amount of antirust ingredient that had been featured in the advertisements; apparently the manufacturer had decided to *adulterate* the paint with mineral oil.

2. **condescend** (kon di SEND)

   a. Dr. Walton is not the most popular doctor at the hospital because he gives the impression that he will *condescend* to speak only to those nurses who assist him in surgery.
   b. Do you think Kurt will *condescend* to speak to us now that he has inherited a fortune?

3. **dissipate** (DIS ə pāt)

   a. Potentially outstanding musicians sometimes *dissipate* rather than develop their talent because they are unwilling to practice sufficiently.
   b. Our basketball team, which practiced extra hard all week, was determined not to *dissipate* its opportunity to clinch the league title.

4. **expedite** (EK spi dīt)

   a. To *expedite* matters, Roxanne planned all the details of her camping trip a month in advance.
   b. The Gibrans contributed another fifty thousand dollars to *expedite* the completion of the new church.

5. **inhibit** (in HIB it)

   a. Crescent City's Chamber of Commerce maintains that the raising of property taxes would *inhibit* the economic growth of the city.
   b. If you don't stop criticizing everything Megan says, you will *inhibit* her efforts to overcome her feelings of inferiority.

6. refute (ri FŪT)

    a. Even if one doesn't care for sports, it is hard to *refute* the prominent role sports play in American society.

    b. I don't understand how Uncle Angus can *refute* my claim that he watches too much television as he can generally be found in front of the set.

7. subjugate (SUB jə gat)

    a. Hitler used his superior military forces to *subjugate* the countries bordering Germany.

    b. The dictator resorted to torture, murder, and other inhumane tactics in his attempt to *subjugate* all opposition.

8. terminate (TUR mə nāt)

    a. Unless business improves, company officials will *terminate* plans to expand the size of the plant.

    b. The chairperson attempted to *terminate* the discussion.

9. usurp (ū SURP)

    a. Parents should be careful that they do not *usurp* their children's rights to make certain decisions.

    b. When Mr. Phelps, assistant editor of the paper, attempted to *usurp* authority that rightfully belonged only to the editor-in-chief, the reporters protested.

10. utilize (Ū tə līz)

    a. If you have a complaint about the company supplying oil to your home, you should *utilize* your right to contact the state's Public Utilities Commission.

    b. I think you could *utilize* your speaking ability in sales work.

EXERCISES FOR LESSON 20
Verbs: action words

I. *Directions:* Match each definition to the word part it defines.

_____	1. adulterate	**a.**	to prove false, to deny the truth or accuracy of
_____	2. condescend	**b.**	to restrain, hinder, or check
_____	3. dissipate	**c.**	to make impure, to debase with inferior ingredients
_____	4. expedite	**d.**	to end, to conclude, to finish
_____	5. inhibit	**e.**	to waste, to squander
_____	6. refute	**f.**	to seize control
_____	7. subjugate	**g.**	to descend to a less formal or dignified level, to assume an air of superiority
_____	8. terminate	**h.**	to put to use, to make use of
_____	9. usurp	**i.**	to conquer, to overpower
_____	10. utilize	**j.**	to speed up the progress, to hasten

II. *Directions:* In each space, write the appropriate word from those listed below.

adulterate	dissipate	inhibit	subjugate	usurp
condescend	expedite	refute	terminate	utilize

1. Jeanne refuses to take formal music lessons because she fears that such lessons might _____ her natural ability.

2. We were able to _____ the project because of our vast experience.

3. Gary resolved to _____ his smoking when his doctor told him, "Gary, the x-rays of your lungs look like those of a person who has worked in coal mines for years."

4. Since Brad started going with his latest girlfriend, he will seldom _____ to spend an evening bowling with his old teammates.

5. One technique that you can _____ in attempting to understand a word's meaning is to study the context in which the word appears.

6. Briana feels that she will _____ the day unless she studies for three hours, exercises for an hour, and practices on her guitar for a half-hour.

7. History repeatedly reveals that when a strong country attempts to _____ its weaker neighbors, war is the inevitable result.

8. It was shocking to discover that a meat company would actually _____ its hamburger with horse meat.

9. The janitor did not intend to _____ the teacher's authority, but when the bell rang, he ordered the students to their room.

10. Forrest is very opposed to movie censorship although he can't _____ Hope's claim that too much violence is being featured in some of today's films.

III. *Directions:* Write *Yes* in the space if the italicized word is used correctly, *No* if it is not.

_____ 1. The most popular character in the television series *Dallas* is J.R., an *adulterate* husband and an unscrupulous businessman.

_____ 2. Grandfather said that he enjoyed his first flight except when the turbulence would make the plane *condescend*.

_____ 3. My geology professor said he would *dissipate* the assignment at the end of the next class session so that everyone would know what he or she was to do.

_____ 4. The mayor said that the proposed bridge will *expedite* traffic flow through the city because it will help reduce the congestion on the east side.

_____ 5. After eating the hot, spicy chili, Ruth's bubbling stomach seemed to *inhibit* her ability to breathe.

_____ 6. Mr. Sobieski's remarks about the need for modernizing the community hospital were so persuasive that only one person attempted to *refute* his comments.

_____ 7. The postal clerk said that I would have to *subjugate* the package before it could be mailed overseas.

         8. Francesca decided to *terminate* her dance lessons because she couldn't seem to find enough time to practice.

         9. Buzz enjoyed the plane ride until it made a sudden, *usurp* dive.

         10. Bart was able to *utilize* his mechanical skills to find a job at a gas station.

IV. *Directions:* After selecting your response, put the letter that is before it in the space provided.

    1. Subjugate is associated with
      a. studying
      b. subduing
      c. sweetening

    2. The word closest in meaning to **usurp** is
      a. trespass
      b. resemble
      c. fascinate

    3. The *opposite* of **dissipate** is
      a. vanish
      b. preserve
      c. disperse

    4. The *opposite* of **refute** is
      a. concede
      b. disapprove
      c. repudiate

    5. Terminate: index ::
      a. finish : chapter
      b. start : publisher
      c. introduce : preface

    6. Inhibit : muzzle ::
      a. reassure : confide
      b. repress : smother
      c. restrain : promote

_____ 7. **Adulterate** : purify ::
   a. advance : retreat
   b. adopt : choose
   c. adore : worship

_____ 8. **Utilize** : employ ::
   a. use : neglect
   b. disregard : ignore
   c. execute : intervene

_____ 9. If you **expedite** something, you are concerned with
   a. profit
   b. efficiency
   c. yield

_____ 10. **Condescend** suggests
   a. high to low
   b. heavy to light
   c. half to whole

Verbs: action words

1. **alleviate** (ə LĒ vē āt)

   a. Despite staggering obstacles, many people are working to *alleviate* world hunger.
   b. The trainer was able to *alleviate* the player's pain by applying an ice bag to the swollen ankle.

2. **allude** (ə LOOD)

   a. Did Emil, who wants to be a veterinarian, *allude* to the fact that he had grown up on a farm?
   b. At first, Leon would obviously become embarrassed when someone would *allude* to the braces on his teeth. Eventually he realized that many of his acquaintances wore or had worn braces also, so he became much less self-conscious about this matter.

3. **corroborate** (kə ROB ə rāt)

   a. Much to the distress of Agatha and her lawyer, the mysterious witness did *corroborate* previous testimony that Agatha did indeed have reason to seek revenge against the victim.
   b. In an attempt to *corroborate* Allan's claim that the Sea Mist Restaurant served the best seafood in town, we took our relatives there for dinner.

4. **debilitate** (di BIL i tāt)

   a. Wilma's doctor warned her that if she continued her fad diet, she might *debilitate* herself to such an extent that she could become seriously ill.
   b. After he accompanied his uncle on a cross-country trip, Glenn concluded that if most truckers led the life his uncle did, then they must *debilitate* their health because of the irregular meals and sleep.

5. **exploit** (ik SPLOIT)

   a. Alexis doesn't want to *exploit* her aunt's good nature by asking her to babysit again.

   b. The Tigers' basketball coach said that his players would have to *exploit* their superior quickness and speed if they were to defeat their much taller opponents.

6. **extricate** (EK strə kāt)

   a. Enrique believes that the only way he can *extricate* his car from the ditch is by calling a tow truck.

   b. After Justin had trouble remembering the names of the host and hostess when he attempted to introduce his wife to them, he quickly decided to *extricate* himself from the embarrassing situation by pretending that he had an important telephone call to make.

7. **garner** (GAR nər)

   a. The president believes that he will *garner* enough voting strength in the South to win reelection.

   b. Did you *garner* anything useful from her long speech?

8. **inundate** (IN ən dāt)

   a. As soon as the game was cut off, protests began to *inundate* the TV station.

   b. Farmers living near the swollen river feared that water would *inundate* their recently planted fields.

9. **mitigate** (MIT ə gāt)

   a. The patient was grateful when the powerful medication finally began to *mitigate* his pain.

   b. The United Nations called an emergency meeting in an effort to *mitigate* the tension existing in the Middle East.

10. **preclude** (pri KLŪD)

    a. Dikran's diabetes does not *preclude* his participation in sports.

    b. Even though ItsuRu has an A average and received an A on her term paper, her history professor said that these grades do not *preclude* her from taking the final examination.

EXERCISES FOR LESSON 21
Verbs: action words

I. *Directions:* Match each definition to the word part it defines.

_____	**1.** alleviate	**a.**	to mention briefly or indirectly
_____	**2.** allude	**b.**	to free from a difficult situation
_____	**3.** corroborate	**c.**	to confirm or substantiate, to make more certain
_____	**4.** debilitate	**d.**	to exclude, prevent, or make unnecessary
_____	**5.** exploit	**e.**	to make less harsh or painful, to calm, soothe
_____	**6.** extricate	**f.**	to make weak or feeble
_____	**7.** garner	**g.**	to overflow or overwhelm
_____	**8.** inundate	**h.**	to take advantage of, to use selfishly for one's own ends
_____	**9.** mitigate	**i.**	to collect, to acquire
_____	**10.** preclude	**j.**	to make easier to endure, to reduce or diminish

II. *Directions:* In each space, write the appropriate word from those listed below.

alleviate	corroborate	exploit	garner	mitigate
allude	debilitate	extricate	inundate	preclude

1. The fact that Marianne has numerous food allergies does _____ her from eating certain desserts.

2. Vera's history teacher told the class that most ancient Romans would not bathe frequently because they believed that too many baths would _____ their bodies.

3. Holly believes that soccer will _____ more popularity in the United States within the next few years.

4. Mack was able to _____ his money worries after he got a much better paying job.

5. The overflow from the creek began to _____ the road at the bottom of Manassas Hill after the heavy rains.

6. The janitor in our building never did _____ to the fact that he had been decorated for bravery in World War II.

7. The arrival of food, medicines, clothes, and other supplies began to _____ the desperate conditions existing at the refugee camp.

8. Al had a headache, so he decided to _____ himself from the kitchen when one of the other waiters and the cook got into a bad argument.

9. Jillian decided to _____ with the police officer the directions to the baseball stadium she had been given by the young attendant at the gas station.

10. Mercer was able to _____ his ability to speak and write in several languages into a government career overseas.

III. *Directions:* Write *Yes* in the space if the italicized word is used correctly, *No* if it is not.

_____ 1. To *alleviate* his grandmother's injured feelings because he had forgotten to send her a birthday card, Joel took her to dinner.

_____ 2. Perhaps if you would *allude* your coffee with cream, you wouldn't have such difficulty falling asleep at night.

_____ 3. The paneling in the den was made of *corroborate* material, not wood.

_____ 4. To make our small room look larger, the paint store manager suggested that we paint the room a bold, *debilitate* color.

_____ 5. When he saw the immense congregation, the visiting minister decided to *exploit* his knowledge of world hunger by presenting information that would encourage people to become involved in combatting this staggering problem.

_____ 6. Phil never felt comfortable among his loud-talking uncles and their families, so he decided to *extricate* himself from the family reunion as soon as possible.

_____ 7. The glitter of the moonlight on the lake and the *garner* of the breeze through the pine trees inspired Tiff to write a love letter to his girlfriend.

_____ **8.** Unless the state environmental agency grants permission
to use a stronger pesticide, the gypsy moth will *inundate*
our region again.

_____ **9.** My Aunt Molly's house, an old Victorian located at the
end of the block, had a *mitigate* and balcony running
around the second story in the back, where my brothers
and sisters and I used to play pirates.

_____ **10.** The city council intends to *preclude* a comprehensive
recreational program because it is felt that all citizens
should have an opportunity to enjoy the facilities and
programs throughout the community.

IV. *Directions:* After selecting your response, put the letter that is before it in
the space provided.

_____ **1.** Which of the following would most likely **debilitate** a person?
  a. nourishment
  b. disease
  c. humor

_____ **2.** The person who would most likely **mitigate** a tense situation is a
  a. police officer
  b. bystander
  c. criminal

_____ **3.** Which word is most closely associated with **alleviate**?
  a. afflict
  b. banish
  c. console

_____ **4.** **Inundate** : withhold ::
  a. wilt : blossom
  b. witness : verify
  c. crackle : pop

_____ **5.** **Exploit** : profit ::
  a. utilize : practice
  b. manipulate : benefit
  c. use : retire

_____ **6. Allude** : hint ::
  a. alter : maintain
  b. persuade : discourage
  c. connect : attach

_____ **7. Corroborate** : witness ::
  a. laws : judge
  b. defend : lawyer
  c. obligation : police officer

_____ **8.** The *opposite* of to **extricate** is to
  a. degenerate
  b. succeed
  c. restrain

_____ **9.** The *opposite* of to **preclude** is to
  a. support
  b. modernize
  c. advertise

_____ **10.** Which of the following would most likely be **garnered**?
  a. grain
  b. hair
  c. illness

Verbs: action words

1. **ameliorate** (ə MĒL yə rāt)

   a. Glenda hoped to *ameliorate* the tense situation that existed between her and her roommate by being more thoughtful and understanding.

   b. Henry joined the Peace Corps in an effort to *ameliorate* the living conditions of those less fortunate than he.

2. **assimilate** (ə SIM ə lāt)

   a. As might be expected, it generally does not take a child as long to *assimilate* a new culture as it does his or her parents.

   b. "At this time of day," George remarked, "I find it extremely difficult to *assimilate* all the information that the computer puts forth."

3. **attest** (ə TEST)

   a. I'm sure that Malcolm's sister, who is in her third year of law school, would *attest* to the fact that English is an appropriate major for a college student planning on a legal career.

   b. The producers had no trouble in finding a popular basketball player to *attest* to the refreshing taste of the soft drink.

4. **augment** (og MENT)

   a. Mr. Lobez works three mornings a week at the Colonial Bookstore to *augment* his retirement income.

   b. The mayor strove to *augment* her power by means of undermining her opponents.

5. **chasten** (CHĀ sən)

   a. Most of the students appreciate the fact that Betsy, the head resident, will *chasten* anyone who fails to observe quiet hours.

   b. When her husband continued to defy his doctor's orders to lose weight, Mrs. Sevenson felt compelled to *chasten* him by refusing to bake any more desserts.

133

6. **disseminate** (di SEM ə nāt)

   a. A major purpose of the National Health Institute is to *disseminate* information beneficial to the well-being of the American people.
   b. College had been such a struggle for Timothy that he wanted to *disseminate* news of his graduation to everyone he knew.

7. **embroil** (em BROIL)

   a. Amy's grandparents said they did not want to *embroil* themselves in a family dispute when Amy asked them to help persuade her parents to let her buy a car.
   b. Murray did not want to *embroil* himself in gossip about his neighbors, so he quickly changed the subject.

8. **expunge** (ik SPUNJ)

   a. If Melissa gets higher grades for the courses that she is repeating, the registrar will *expunge* the lower grades from her transcript.
   b. The judge announced that he had decided to *expunge* the witness's inappropriate remarks from the court records.

9. **harass** (HAR əs)

   a. Some members of the audience would *harass* the speaker by shouting insults at him.
   b. The mayor obviously felt that the reporter was trying to *harass* him by repeatedly asking questions about his personal life.

10. **infuse** (in FŪS)

    a. Of all the presidents in the twentieth century, perhaps none could *infuse* the country with more pride and confidence than the Roosevelts: Theodore (president from 1901 to 1909) and Franklin (president from 1933 to 1945).
    b. The conductor told the orchestra members that they must *infuse* their playing with more feeling.

EXERCISES FOR LESSON 22
Verbs: action words

I. *Directions:* Match each definition to the word part it defines.

_____ **1.** ameliorate   **a.** to blend in, to absorb, to incorporate as one's own

_____ **2.** assimilate   **b.** to bring into conflict, to involve in a struggle

_____ **3.** attest   **c.** to discipline, to punish for the purpose of moral improvement

_____ **4.** augment   **d.** to inspire with feelings, to fill with

_____ **5.** chasten   **e.** to torment, to persecute, to trouble by repeated attacks

_____ **6.** disseminate   **f.** to increase, to supplement

_____ **7.** embroil   **g.** to improve, to make better

_____ **8.** expunge   **h.** to scatter or spread widely

_____ **9.** harass   **i.** to erase, to blot out

_____ **10.** infuse   **j.** to bear witness to, to certify

II. *Directions:* In each space, write the appropriate word from those listed below.

ameliorate	attest	chasten	embroil	harass
assimilate	augment	disseminate	expunge	infuse

1. Because Ashley had fulfilled the terms of her parole, the judge decided to _____ the misdemeanors from her record.

2. Mr. LeClair purchased newspaper space and radio time to _____ the news that his furniture store would be moving to a new location.

3. The prosecuting attorney asked if there were any witnesses who could _____ to her whereabouts on the day of the crime.

4. Geena would often _____ her boyfriend about his low-paying job, so he eventually broke up with her.

5. The newly elected mayor pledged to _____ housing conditions for the elderly.

6. I don't want to _____ you in my problem, but don't you think my employer should pay for the computer course I have to take to do my job?

7. The coach tried to _____ the team with more spirit by reminding them how badly their opponents had defeated them last year.

8. Astronauts must be able to _____ highly technical information.

9. You were correct to _____ Jason for running into the street without looking.

10. Miguel was able to _____ his already impressive muscles by working on the universal machine three times a week.

III. *Directions:* Write *Yes* in the space if the italicized word is used correctly, *No* if it is not.

_____ 1. Rob's Pontiac, painted a brilliant *ameliorate* red, was his pride and joy.

_____ 2. Rex has been promoted to chief inspector of the *assimilate* factory.

_____ 3. Farahnaz believes that the computer data will *attest* to the validity of her theory.

_____ 4. Paolo decided to *augment* his savings for his European trip by taking a nighttime security job at the airport.

_____ 5. Tippi watched the pigeons *chasten* the popcorn she threw in their direction.

_____ 6. The state has hired a public relations agency to *disseminate* information about the outstanding employment opportunities that exist in its major cities.

_____ 7. You should *embroil* the hot dogs for at least seven minutes before serving them.

_____ 8. The temperature's sudden *expunge* was due to a large cold front that had unexpectedly moved into the area.

_____ 9. Some unruly fans began to *harass* the star baseball player after he had struck out for the second time.

_____ 10. Abe has the respect of his friends because they know he will not *infuse* even one drink if he is going to drive later.

IV. *Directions:* After selecting your response, put the letter that is before it in the space provided.

_____ 1. **Embroil** suggests
     a. imagination
     b. involvement
     c. irregularity

_____ 2. The person most likely to be **chastened** is one who is
     a. corrupt
     b. ill
     c. prosperous

_____ 3. Something that is **disseminated** is certainly *not*
     a. circulated
     b. complicated
     c. concealed

_____ 4. **Infuse** : inspire ::
     a. reason : influence
     b. lecture : recite
     c. fasten : unlatch

_____ 5. **Expunge** : explain ::
     a. delete : omit
     b. erase : clarify
     c. blot : expire

_____ 6. **Harass** : enemy ::
     a. encourage : ally
     b. participate : amateur
     c. contribute : recipient

_____ 7. **Augment** : expand ::
     a. rupture : repair
     b. bonus : earn
     c. magnify : heighten

_____ 8. Most people would most likely try to **ameliorate**
     a. problems
     b. directions
     c. miracles

_____ 9. **Assimilate** suggests that something will be
   a. absorbed
   b. betrayed
   c. captivated

_____ 10. The *opposite* of **attest** is
   a. contradict
   b. reward
   c. murmur

Verbs: action words

1. <u>ad</u>monish (ad MON ish)

   a. Randy's biology professor had to *admonish* him for being continually late for the laboratory sessions.
   b. The pediatrician advised the parents at the meeting not to *admonish* their children if they didn't eat all the food on their plates, as it was more than likely that they were getting adequate nutrition.

2. cull (KUL)

   a. Dan volunteered to *cull* appropriate yearbook photos from the stack of campus newspapers.
   b. Nancy continued to *cull* overripe tomatoes from the display counter.

3. discern (di SURN)

   a. Jeff could sense that Micaela was angry with him, but he could not *discern* from her remarks why she was.
   b. I could *discern* from Sally's expression that she was surprised by the news.

4. enhance (en HANS)

   a. Ned quit smoking and started jogging to *enhance* his health.
   b. Seth helped to *enhance* his employment prospects by taking a couple of computer courses.

5. feign (FĀN)

   a. The professional pianist confessed that as a child he would sometimes *feign* illness to escape from going to a piano lesson.
   b. Although Kevin had never been interested in fishing, he decided to *feign* an interest in this sport to please his grandfather, a dedicated fisherman.

6. **inculcate** (in KUL kāt)

   a. The instructor tried to *inculcate* an appreciation for classical music by playing Beethoven symphonies twice a week.
   b. To *inculcate* a respect for the safety rules is a major responsibility of the factory supervisors.

7. **intimidate** (in TIM i dāt)

   a. After practicing on the intermediate ski slopes, Arlene decided not to let the expert slopes *intimidate* her anymore.
   b. The Key Bar's muscular bouncer can easily *intimidate* any unruly customer by a mere glance.

8. **perpetuate** (pər PECH ū āt)

   a. Because of increased costs, our college considered ending its overseas study opportunities, but a corporation's generous gift has enabled the college to *perpetuate* this program.
   b. An eternal flame at President John F. Kennedy's grave serves to *perpetuate* his memory.

9. **procrastinate** (prō KRAS tə nāt)

   a. Brady continued to *procrastinate* applying for the job he saw advertised in the morning paper. When he finally did apply, he was told that someone had been hired earlier.
   b. College students who *procrastinate* their work often panic when the end of the semester rolls around.

10. **repudiate** (ri PŪ dē āt)

    a. Pamela believes that Dr. Wilson, professor of sociology, will *repudiate* your claim that there are more social and recreational opportunities in a large city than in a small town.
    b. The senator is confident that his voting record will *repudiate* his opponent's charge that he is no friend of environmentalists.

EXERCISES FOR LESSON 23
Verbs: action words

I. *Directions:* Match each definition to the word part it defines.

_____ **1.** admonish   **a.** to reject as untrue or unjust

_____ **2.** cull   **b.** to fake, to pretend

_____ **3.** discern   **c.** to continue without interruption, to sustain

_____ **4.** enhance   **d.** to warn, to caution

_____ **5.** feign   **e.** to threaten, to frighten

_____ **6.** inculcate   **f.** to delay, to put off

_____ **7.** intimidate   **g.** to see, to understand

_____ **8.** perpetuate   **h.** to intensify or magnify, to raise to a higher degree

_____ **9.** procrastinate   **i.** to pick out from others, to select

_____ **10.** repudiate   **j.** to influence, to indoctrinate, to impress or teach through earnest repetition

II. *Directions:* In each space, write the appropriate word from those listed below.

| admonish | discern | feign | intimidate | procrastinate |
| cull | enhance | inculcate | perpetuate | repudiate |

1. Beatrice often wears clothes with vertical stripes in an effort to _____ her height.

2. The judge sternly warned the bill collector never again to _____ a person owing an overdue bill.

3. The pharmaceutical company had to _____ its advertising claim that its particular pain reliever was the most effective arthritis medicine available.

4. The young couple never did _____ that the reason people moved away from them during the movie was because of the noisy way they chomped their popcorn.

5. Alvin continued to _____ going to the dentist until the pain became unbearable.

6. Tyler had to _____ the duplicates from his record collection to save space.

7. Ms. Bates took steps to _____ the memory of her late father by establishing a generous scholarship at his alma mater.

8. Some parents had to _____ their young children to be quiet during the long church service.

9. Principal Brownstein constantly attempts to _____ in the students a pride in their community, their school, and themselves.

10. The little girl's father would _____ surprise and fright when she jumped from behind a tree and yelled, "Boo!"

III. *Directions:* Write *Yes* in the space if the italicized word is used correctly, *No* if it is not.

_____ 1. It seemed cruel for the waitress to *admonish* the embarrassed busboy for breaking a glass.

_____ 2. The plumber exclaimed, "I think you have a lot of *cull* for asking me to reduce your bill!"

_____ 3. The personnel manager had a difficult time deciding which applicant to hire since he could not *discern* any major differences in their qualifications.

_____ 4. Mr. Clement did *enhance* his popularity in the community by generously donating both his money and his time to any worthwhile cause.

_____ 5. The ride on the ferris wheel thrilled the little girl, but her father felt *feign*.

_____ 6. To *inculcate* yourself in case it rains, take along this umbrella.

_____ 7. Rosemary and Sidney began having *intimidate* conversations as their affection for one another grew.

_____ 8. Regina wished to *perpetuate* the good relations she had established with her in-laws, so she asked them over for New Year's dinner.

_____ **9.** Marc attempted to *procrastinate* after his boss directed him to begin the supply room inventory, but he was told to quit stalling and to get the work completed.

_____ **10.** Ellis, a professional baseball player as well as a medical student, could certainly *repudiate* the myth that athletes are all brawn and no brains.

IV. *Directions:* After selecting your response, put the letter that is before it in the space provided.

_____ **1. Perpetuate** suggests
   a. continuation
   b. postponement
   c. termination

_____ **2. Repudiate** suggests
   a. reaction
   b. rejection
   c. reproduction

_____ **3. Procrastinate** suggests
   a. delay
   b. intrigue
   c. prediction

_____ **4.** The *opposite* of to **cull** is to
   a. abandon
   b. burden
   c. choose

_____ **5. Intimidate** : wrong ::
   a. associate : mistake
   b. encourage : correct
   c. inquire : investigate

_____ **6. Discern** : helpful ::
   a. recover : profitable
   b. detect : beneficial
   c. achieve : workable

_____ **7. Admonish** : caution ::
  a. adjourn : discontinue
  b. adjust : disarrange
  c. administer : distinguish

_____ **8. Enhance** : attractiveness ::
  a. elegant : handsome
  b. esteem : beautiful
  c. exalt : loveliness

_____ **9.** Which animal is associated with **feign**?
  a. giraffe
  b. opossum
  c. shark

_____ **10.** Which word is most closely associated with **inculcate**?
  a. implant
  b. immobile
  c. imminent

Adjectives: descriptive words

1. **belated** (bi LĀ tid)

   a. Ashamed of herself for having forgotten the date, Eleanor had to send a *belated* anniversary card to her grandparents.

   b. Herschel was disappointed, but not surprised, that his *belated* apology was not accepted.

2. **candid** (KAN did)

   a. Unlike Fred, who often beats around the bush, Casimir always gives you his *candid* opinion when you ask.

   b. Cornelia maintains that she was merely being *candid* when she expressed her opinions about Brenda's singing, but others thought that she had been quite insensitive.

3. **decadent** (DEK ə dənt)

   a. Historians believe that the *decadent* behavior of the ancient Romans contributed to the downfall of the Roman Empire.

   b. The motel units were in *decadent* condition; all needed to be painted, most needed air conditioners, some had broken windows.

4. **eclectic** (e KLEK tik)

   a. The government has adopted an *eclectic* approach rather than a single approach in attempting to solve the unemployment problem.

   b. Ms. Henderson's *eclectic* teaching techniques, ranging from individual instruction to class field trips, result in impressive scholastic achievements by her students.

5. **fetid** (FET id)

   a. A *fetid* odor greeted the family when the campsite was finally reached.

   b. A bag of *fetid* potatoes was rotting on the basement floor.

6. languid (LANG gwid)

a. After being unable to sleep during the night, Cindy felt *languid* the next day.

b. The children behaved in a *languid* manner after sitting around and watching television steadily for three hours.

7. naive (na ĒV)

a. Earl seems to be an intelligent person, but his political philosophy strikes me as being *naive*.

b. I can't believe that Lauren is so *naive* that she actually believes the way to balance the nation's budget is simply to print more money.

8. palatable (PAL ətə bəl)

a. The company was enjoyable, the music soothing, and the food *palatable*; Gopal had a wonderful time.

b. Freda quit her job because all the traveling that was required was not *palatable* to her.

9. tacit (TAS it)

a. Pierre and Louise never discussed politics. Apparently, they had come to a *tacit* agreement that this was a subject that they could never agree upon.

b. After the coach emphasized the importance of reporting to practice in top condition next month, the players reached a *tacit* understanding that they had better start immediately working out by themselves.

10. wary (WĀR ē)

a. Many people are obviously *wary* about further development of nuclear energy.

b. I'm *wary* of people who gossip all the time. I suspect that they talk about me when I'm not around!

EXERCISES FOR LESSON 24
Adjectives: descriptive words

I. *Directions:* Match each definition to the word part it defines.

_____ 1. belated

_____ 2. candid

_____ 3. decadent

_____ 4. eclectic

_____ 5. fetid

_____ 6. languid

_____ 7. naive

_____ 8. palatable

_____ 9. tacit

_____ 10. wary

a. implied, understood without being openly expressed

b. lacking energy, sluggish

c. cautious, on one's guard

d. various, from many sources

e. satisfactory, pleasing to the taste

f. late, coming after the expected time

g. frank, open and sincere

h. unsophisticated, unsuspecting

i. having an offensive odor, stinking

j. decline, deterioration

II. *Directions:* In each space, write the appropriate word from those listed below.

| belated | decadent | fetid | naive | tacit |
| candid | eclectic | languid | palatable | wary |

1. My roommate was _____ for weeks after he had a bout with the flu, but he eventually recovered his strength and energy.

2. We had a _____ agreement that whoever got home first would begin preparing supper.

3. Community leaders realized that steps had to be taken to combat the _____ conditions that had developed in various areas of the city.

4. Patrick thought he would like pecan pie, but because of its richness, the pie was simply not _____ to him.

5. The new postman is _____ of our dog; he always keeps his eye on Sheena whenever he delivers mail.

6. Though his rudeness had occurred over a month ago, Derek's _____ apology was graciously accepted by his landlord.

7. I may be _____ to ask, but did you really run in two marathons over the weekend?

8. Santha has _____ movie preferences, ranging from old-fashioned romances to science fiction.

9. My compost pile gives off a _____ odor, but I know the material in it will provide good fertilizer for my garden next spring.

10. Mrs. LaValle's _____ remarks about the good and bad features of the houses she sells surprise some potential buyers, but they do appreciate her frankness.

III. *Directions:* Write *Yes* in the space if the italicized word is used correctly, *No* if it is not.

_____ 1. After two years of poor crops, the people were *belated* by this season's bountiful harvest.

_____ 2. In addition to turkey and pumpkin pie, I look forward to the *candid* sweet potatoes my aunt always makes for Thanksgiving dinner.

_____ 3. The downtown movie theater, which has been in *decadent* condition for years, will soon be remodeled.

_____ 4. On the advice of my mechanic, I bought a new *eclectic* starter for my car.

_____ 5. Charlotte believes that the *fetid* odor from the river is due to chemical wastes.

_____ 6. Near the coast, *languid* sea gulls drifted lazily in the sky.

_____ 7. The *naive* in Rachel's neck had been hurt in the accident, but the doctor assured her that she would make a complete recovery.

_____ 8. Many students complain about the dorm's food, but I think it is quite *palatable*.

_____ 9. A *tacit* understanding soon existed between the sergeant and his men; they knew that the barracks had to be spotless before any weekend passes would be issued.

_____ **10.** Gayle is sometimes *wary* when she is introduced to strangers, but after a while she generally relaxes and enjoys their company.

IV. *Directions:* After selecting your response, put the letter that is before it in the space provided.

____ **1. Eclectic** suggests
   a. awareness
   b. broadness
   c. clearness

____ **2. Tacit** suggests that something is
   a. expensive
   b. implied
   c. threatening

____ **3.** Which word would you associate with **palatable**?
   a. agreeable
   b. bitterness
   c. criticize

____ **4.** You would expect a **naive** person to be
   a. experienced
   b. unsuspecting
   c. peculiar

____ **5. Wary** : suspicious ::
   a. alert : alarming
   b. watchful : attentive
   c. cautious : heedless

____ **6. Belated** : slowpoke ::
   a. prompt : Johnny-on-the-spot
   b. timely : Johnny-come-lately
   c. tardy : Johnny-be-good

____ **7. Decadent** : upward ::
   a. decline : rise
   b. ruin : downward
   c. modern : slope

_____ 8. **Candid** : honesty ::
   a. honor : praising
   b. deceptive : fraud
   c. frank : deceit

_____ 9. A **languid** person is certainly *not*
   a. forceful
   b. lazy
   c. exhausted

_____ 10. Which word would you associate with **fetid**?
   a. haunted
   b. attracted
   c. spoiled

Adjectives: descriptive words

1. <u>chronic</u> (KRON ik)

   a. Because he was troubled with a *chronic* backache, Graham reluctantly quit his job as a milkman.
   b. The doctor said that the *chronic* headache Allen had throughout the winter was caused by a sinus infection.

2. <u>conducive</u> (kən DOO siv)

   a. Tamar's positive attitude throughout her ordeal, the doctor stated, had been *conducive* to her full recovery.
   b. The excitement and stimulation of city life were *conducive* to his creativity, the artist maintained.

3. **imperative** (im PER ə tive)

   a. The president said that it was *imperative* to help the refugees begin life anew in our country.
   b. Priscilla realizes that it is *imperative* for her to practice a minimum of four hours daily if she is to become a concert pianist.

4. **latent** (LĀT ənt)

   a. Her *latent* abilities as a writer were not developed until she was fifty years old.
   b. Cynthia capitalized on her *latent* artistic ability by painting every chance she got; as a result, her skills improved.

5. <u>malignant</u> (mə LIG nənt)

   a. Mr. Lorenson was overjoyed to learn that his tumor was not *malignant*.
   b. Tragically, four people became victims of the *malignant* gas that was accidentally released.

6. **parochial** (pə RŌ kē əl)

   a. To be a diplomat, one needs to have broad rather than *parochial* perspectives.
   b. An elderly neighbor of mine talks only about his garden and baseball, but despite his *parochial* interests, I enjoy talking with him.

7. **perfunctory** (pər FUNK tə rē)

   a. Rodney enjoyed the concert, but because his favorite band played without enthusiasm, he was disappointed with its *perfunctory* performance.
   b. Whiz, the Caldwell's dog, made only a brief, *perfunctory* sniff at the trembling puppy, then continued on his jaunt through the neighborhood.

8. **precocious** (pri KŌ shəs)

   a. Mozart was a *precocious* child; he was giving piano performances and composing music before he was ten years old.
   b. My grandfather thinks his three-year-old grandson is *precocious* because he can count to fifty, but I don't think that ability is unusual for a child of that age.

9. **sordid** (SOR did)

   a. The *sordid* details of Allie's private life jeopardized her chances for reelection.
   b. The governor pledged that migrant workers would never again be forced to endure *sordid* working conditions, such as being housed in abandoned old railroad boxcars.

10. **variable** (VAR ē əbəl)

    a. During our vacation, we had *variable* weather, from rain and fog to sunny and cloudless days.
    b. Aram certainly has *variable* interests, as shown by his dedication to stamp collecting and skydiving.

EXERCISES FOR LESSON 25
Adjectives: descriptive words

I. *Directions:* Match each definition to the word part it defines.

_____ **1.** chronic	**a.** disgraceful, filthy, squalid
_____ **2.** conducive	**b.** continuing, of long duration
_____ **3.** imperative	**c.** deadly, lethal, harmful
_____ **4.** latent	**d.** tending to help or assist
_____ **5.** malignant	**e.** changeable
_____ **6.** parochial	**f.** performed in an uninteresting or routine manner
_____ **7.** perfunctory	**g.** limited or narrow in viewpoint
_____ **8.** precocious	**h.** necessary, essential, obligatory
_____ **9.** sordid	**i.** potential, capable of becoming but not now visible
_____ **10.** variable	**j.** advanced in the mind or skills at an early age

II. *Directions:* In each space, write the appropriate word from those listed below.

chronic	imperative	malignant	perfunctory	sordid
conducive	latent	parochial	precocious	variable

1. At the age of seven, Dane displayed _____ ability to handle the numerous chores associated with operating the farm.

2. My sociology professor said that it is _____ that we all attend class this Friday if we want to know what will be included on the final exam.

3. Greed can become so _____ that it can destroy families as well as friendships.

4. Gina's disposition is so _____ that she can be joking one minute and serious the next.

5. Paying bills on time is certainly _____ to a good credit rating.

6. When the copilot made a casual check of the plane before takeoff, the pilot lectured him sternly for making such a _____ inspection.

7. Melinda's parents believe that she has _____ athletic ability, so they have hired an instructor to give her ice skating lessons.

8. The Walters, a retired couple, are anything but _____ in their interests as they enjoy traveling, attending symphony concerts, refinishing furniture, bowling, and canoeing.

9. Most people don't enjoy being around a _____ complainer because the constant complaining becomes tiresome and depressing.

10. Every soap opera seems to have at least one major character who leads a _____ life—a life full of deception, infidelity, and crime.

III. *Directions:* Write *Yes* in the space if the italicized word is used correctly, *No* if it is not.

_____ 1. Since Felia moved to the city, she's had a *chronic* eye problem because of the smog.

_____ 2. The symphony orchestra concluded its concert with a classical piece from the *conducive* period.

_____ 3. My doctor thinks it is *imperative* that I have a yearly physical examination.

_____ 4. Although Clifford did not seem to be blessed with *latent* musical ability, his many hours of practice made him a better-than-average guitarist.

_____ 5. Lions display *malignant* behavior when they are provoked.

_____ 6. The prisoner was given a *parochial* for good behavior.

_____ 7. Being tired, Mr. Moreno made only a *perfunctory* effort to sell the insurance policy, so he was surprised when the newlyweds readily agreed to buy the policy.

_____ 8. Because the crystal set is so *precocious*, the appraiser advised Mrs. Kline to have it insured.

_____ 9. When spring finally came, the trees seemed to blossom overnight with beautiful, *sordid* leaves.

_____ **10.** The *variable* winds made it difficult for the sailboats to make steady progress.

IV. *Directions:* After selecting your response, put the letter that is before it in the space provided.

_____ **1. Variable** is associated with
   a. determining
   b. coordinating
   c. shifting

_____ **2. Perfunctory** suggests
   a. apathy
   b. sympathy
   c. therapy

_____ **3. Latent** suggests
   a. potential
   b. success
   c. bordering

_____ **4. Malignant** : distress ::
   a. harmless : joy
   b. mistreat : cherish
   c. interest : boredom

_____ **5. Conducive** : hazardous ::
   a. manipulative : threatening
   b. contributive : dangerous
   c. restrictive : perilous

_____ **6. Sordid** : honorable ::
   a. noble : lofty
   b. sorrow : grief
   c. dirty : clean

_____ **7. Chronic** : persistent ::
   a. constant : seldom
   b. giggling : laughing
   c. occasionally : frequently

_____ **8.** The *opposite* of **imperative** is
    a. aware
    b. unnecessary
    c. urgent

_____ **9.** A **parochial** person is certainly *not* considered
    a. ambitious
    b. tolerant
    c. petty

_____ **10.** At what age is someone most likely to be **precocious**?
    a. ten
    b. thirty
    c. sixty

Adjectives: descriptive words

1. **banal** (bə NAL or BĀ nəl)

   a. The mystery movie lacked originality in all respects—it contained typical characters, *banal* dialogue, and a predictable plot.

   b. Because Greg thought the activities available on campus during the weekends were generally boring and *banal*, he often went home.

2. **benevolent** (bə NEV ə lənt)

   a. Gloria is a *benevolent* person; she is constantly devoting her time and money to others.

   b. The Michauds' *benevolent* acts for the elderly neighbors earned them the respect of the entire community.

3. **clandestine** (klan DES tən)

   a. Unknown to the public, the general manager and coach of the professional basketball team held a number of *clandestine* meetings about whether or not to trade their star player.

   b. A small group of citizens held *clandestine* assemblies to plot the overthrow of the repressive government.

4. **cogent** (KŌ jənt)

   a. There are many legitimate reasons for not smoking, but those having to do with health are the most *cogent*.

   b. The newlyweds bought the nine-passenger van after Mr. Downey presented them with a number of *cogent* reasons for doing so.

5. **equitable** (EK wi tə bəl)

   a. Representatives for the players and team owners have urged that the contract be approved because they believe the terms are *equitable* for all concerned.

   b. William Vickers was a respected police officer because he treated all citizens in a courteous, *equitable* manner.

6. **indiscreet** (in di SKRĒT)

   a. Do you think it is *indiscreet* of Elizabeth to date a man so much older than she?

   b. It was *indiscreet* of James to ask your husband how much money he makes.

7. **optimistic** (op tə MIS tik)

   a. According to his senate colleagues, Hubert Humphrey was a joy to be around because he was *optimistic* that solutions to the nation's problems could be found.

   b. Giorgio was *optimistic* that he would be hired for the job because of his experience.

8. **tentative** (TENT ə tive)

   a. President Truman was not *tentative* after he made a decision; he took quick, firm action.

   b. Mr. Bryson made a *tentative* offer to buy the house; a final decision depends upon whether the bank approves his loan application.

9. **turgid** (TUR jəd)

   a. X-rays revealed that an intestinal blockage was responsible for the patient's *turgid* abdomen, which had been bloated for two days.

   b. Describing the annual rodeo as "one of America's greatest events" and "unsurpassed in thrills and excitement" are just two examples of the poster's overblown, *turgid* statements.

10. **vehement** (VĒ ə mənt)

   a. Many spectators thought the coach provided a poor example for his players when he engaged in a *vehement* argument with the referees.

   b. Garrison embarrassed his daughter when he made a *vehement* protest to the waiter because of the way the steak had been cooked.

EXERCISES FOR LESSON 26
Adjectives: descriptive words

I. *Directions:* Match each definition to the word part it defines.

_____ **1.** banal   **a.** fair, just and right

_____ **2.** benevolent   **b.** done in secrecy, hidden

_____ **3.** clandestine   **c.** hesitant, uncertain, not final

_____ **4.** cogent   **d.** lacking freshness or originality

_____ **5.** equitable   **e.** furious, passionate, intense

_____ **6.** indiscreet   **f.** generous, charitable

_____ **7.** optimistic   **g.** to the point, appropriate, convincing

_____ **8.** tentative   **h.** swollen, inflated

_____ **9.** turgid   **i.** lacking good judgment, unwise, careless

_____ **10.** vehement   **j.** taking a favorable view, hopeful

II. *Directions:* In each space, write the appropriate word from those listed below.

banal   clandestine   equitable   optimistic   turgid
benevolent   cogent   indiscreet   tentative   vehement

1. Jules says his hockey coach treats all the players in an _____ manner, so everyone gets a chance to play.

2. At social occasions like weddings, it is sometimes difficult to avoid making _____ comments when talking to strangers.

3. The bruised, _____ appearance of Heidi's ankle suggested infection.

4. Stuart is _____ that one of these days he's going to win the Irish Sweepstakes.

5. Historically, Americans have been known as _____ people, helping those in need throughout the world.

6. According to what I heard, the most _____ reason Diana got the job with the band was that she was capable of singing all types of songs, from rock to ballads.

7. Elliott did not generally approve of _____ business meetings, but since he wanted to discuss some sensitive personnel matters, he decided to keep the next meeting secret.

8. Joyce was relieved that her parents made only a mild protest instead of a _____ one when she informed them that she planned to get an apartment of her own.

9. Don't you think it was _____ of you to tell Chad that Ashley is interested in dating him?

10. Leigh's not sure what she will do next fall, but she's made _____ plans to study acting.

III. *Directions:* Write *Yes* in the space if the italicized word is used correctly, *No* if it is not.

_____ 1. Because of the cold temperature and *banal* sun, the mountain climbers postponed their assault on the summit.

_____ 2. Our neighbors brought us some grapefruit from Texas last week, and I've never tasted such *benevolent* fruit.

_____ 3. Mr. Andretti has kept a *clandestine* diary of his prisoner-of-war experiences.

_____ 4. The Coates planted *cogent* trees to mark their property lines.

_____ 5. Most senators stated that they were in favor of cutting taxes if it could be done in an *equitable* way.

_____ 6. Whitney didn't seem to realize that it was *indiscreet* of her to play her stereo so loud at such a late hour.

_____ 7. Even though there was a significant amount of circumstantial evidence against his client, the lawyer was *optimistic* that he would be found innocent.

_____ 8. Gary believed he was often too *tentative* when he attempted to make a sale; he resolved, therefore, to be more confident and assertive.

_____ 9. For their anniversary, Porter bought his wife a *turgid* and had it set in a ring.

_____ **10.** Glancing impatiently at her *vehement* wristwatch, Brandy realized that she still had forty minutes before her plane was due to depart.

IV. *Directions:* After selecting your response, put the letter that is before it in the space provided.

_____ **1. Tentative** suggests a lack of
  a. companionship
  b. confidence
  c. conservation

_____ **2.** Which one is *not* associated with **banal?**
  a. extraordinary
  b. boredom
  c. commonplace

_____ **3. Benevolent** suggests
  a. generosity
  b. feebleness
  c. deception

_____ **4.** A **cogent** person is certainly *not*
  a. positive
  b. unbelievable
  c. compelling

_____ **5. Turgid** : puffy ::
  a. puffy : swollen
  b. swollen : withered
  c. withered: inflated

_____ **6. Optimistic** : bright ::
  a. encouraging : gray
  b. gloomy : dark
  c. cheerful : black

_____ **7. Vehement** : anger ::
  a. passionate : indifference
  b. passive : calm
  c. persuasive : thoughtful

_____ 8. **Equitable** : admirable ::
  a. adjustable : respectable
  b. possible : flexible
  c. fair : praiseworthy

_____ 9. **Indiscreet** : careless ::
  a. careless : careful
  b. careful : cautious
  c. cautious : careworn

_____ 10. **Clandestine** is associated with
  a. calamity
  b. circulation
  c. concealment

Adjectives: descriptive words

1. **adroit** (ə DROIT)

   a. Although she's best known for her skill on the trampoline, Becky is equally *adroit* on the parallel bars.

   b. Kent is *adroit* at juggling, so I've asked him to teach me.

2. **equivocal** (i KWIV ə kəl)

   a. Al has *equivocal* feelings about whether or not to take the vitamin C tablets his wife gave him for his sniffles because he didn't find them particularly helpful in the past.

   b. Buddy has *equivocal* feelings about a job offer to paint houses this summer because he's uncertain he can overcome his fear of heights.

3. **formidable** (FOR mi də bəl)

   a. Thanks to immunization provided by vaccines, polio, a *formidable* disease, can now be prevented.

   b. The *formidable* mountain, which Allwyn and three of his friends had made extensive plans to climb, loomed menacingly before them.

4. **germane** (jər MĀN)

   a. In the interview conducted for the overseas medical position, the most *germane* responses were given by Dr. Harrison; her answers were always convincing and to the point.

   b. Paulette said she wanted to be a carpenter because she loved the smell of wood, which doesn't seem a *germane* reason for choosing this profession.

5. **glib** (GLIB)

   a. I believe the mechanic was just making a *glib* remark when he said that you should sell your car for junk.

   b. Politicians have the reputation for being *glib*, but the truth is that most politicians carefully consider their remarks before speaking in public.

6. **implicit** (im PLIS it)

   a. Although the professor didn't specifically state that we needed to know the physiological terms contained in the chapter, it was *implicit* in his remarks that we should if we expected to do well on the test.
   b. *Implicit* in Ben's silence was his disappointment at the loss.

7. <u>in</u>**exorable** (in EK sər ə bəl)

   a. Nothing could stop the Bears' *inexorable* march to a touchdown.
   b. The mirror cruelly revealed to the aging fashion model the *inexorable* ravages of time.

8. <u>pe</u>**ripheral** (pə RIF ər əl)

   a. Although the film does deal with the personal and social problems associated with alcoholism, it does so only in a *peripheral* way.
   b. Kirstie's off and on, *peripheral* involvement in physical fitness finally ended after she and her husband joined a health club that required them to exercise at least three times a week to maintain their membership.

9. **ultimate** (UL tə mit)

   a. For some adventurous souls, parachute jumping is the *ultimate* sport.
   b. When he was finally able to negotiate the purchase of the radio station, Dominic's *ultimate* dream became a reality.

10. **whimsical** (WIM zi kəl)

    a. Ogden Nash, the poet, is noted for his light, *whimsical* verse.
    b. Feeling in a *whimsical* mood, my brother suddenly decided that he was going to spend the day at the beach rather than at his job in the shoe factory.

EXERCISES FOR LESSON 27
Adjectives: descriptive words

I. *Directions:* Match each definition to the word part it defines.

_____ **1.** adroit

_____ **2.** equivocal

_____ **3.** formidable

_____ **4.** germane

_____ **5.** glib

_____ **6.** implicit

_____ **7.** inexorable

_____ **8.** peripheral

_____ **9.** ultimate

_____ **10.** whimsical

a. maximum, foremost, highest

b. frightful, dreadful, arousing awe

c. given to spur-of-the-moment decisions, impulsive, playful

d. relentless, unyielding, inflexible

e. uncertain, doubtful, questionable

f. implied rather than expressly stated, inferred

g. talkative but insincere or superficial

h. nimble, skillful

i. convincing, compelling, clear and to the point

j. on the outer edge only, on the fringe, not deeply involved

II. *Directions:* In each space, write the appropriate word from those listed below.

| adroit | formidable | glib | inexorable | ultimate |
| equivocal | germane | implicit | peripheral | whimsical |

1. The president was urged to withdraw the nomination, but he stubbornly refused to do so. His _____ position on this matter lost him the support of his own party.

2. I think Mason's sly comments were actually _____ reminders that it was through his efforts that the rest of us got to meet the famous singer.

3. Beatrix's _____ goal is to become a veterinarian as she's always loved animals.

4. Chris just gives offhand, _____ responses when you ask him whether or not he's secretly engaged.

5. Despite presenting every _____ reason he could think of, Jonathan could not get his roommate to change his mind about the matter.

6. Mr. Glover had _____ feelings about whether or not to wear a toupee, but he finally decided he wouldn't.

7. Frost remarked seriously, "When you get to this stage in the Ping-Pong tournament, all of your opponents are _____ ; I'm scared of all of them."

8. Although Marjorie loves to travel, she took only a _____ interest in the geography course she took last semester.

9. Our boss was in a _____ mood today. First, he ordered us to unload the truck, but then he changed his mind and told us to clean up the construction site; about fifteen minutes later, however, he told us to jump into the truck, and we went to a restaurant and had coffee and doughnuts.

10. Mickey is _____ at taking a few eggs and whatever is in the refrigerator and whipping up a delicious meal.

III. *Directions:* Write *Yes* in the space if the italicized word is used correctly, *No* if it is not.

_____ 1. The witness patiently stated to the agitated defense lawyer, "You are very *adroit* at twisting everything I say into something entirely different from what I mean."

_____ 2. Eric found the apartments to be *equivocal*, so he decided to rent the one nearest his job.

_____ 3. President Franklin Roosevelt stated that the most *formidable* foe we have to face is fear itself.

_____ 4. Although Seth is often *glib* when you attempt to talk to him in a serious manner, he can be most insightful at times.

_____ 5. Mr. Turner, an excellent electrician, suggested that I use *implicit* wiring if I wanted indirect lighting in my family room.

_____ 6. The most *germane* reason for requiring writing in college is because good writing contributes to mature thinking.

_____ 7. The many years of working in the coal mines took an *inexorable* toll on Percy's health.

_____ 8. Kelly had only a *peripheral* involvement in the entertainment business; her responsibility was limited to reserving the recording studio for the artists.

_____ 9. Joey experienced the *ultimate* thrill of his life when he was selected as a member of the university's famous marching band.

_____ 10. The *whimsical* french fries were just what the little girl felt like eating.

IV. *Directions:* After selecting your response, put the letter that is before it in the space provided.

____ 1. Which one of these words is associated with **inexorable**?
    a. emotional
    b. relentless
    c. skillful

____ 2. Who has the reputation for being **glib**?
    a. car salesman
    b. chef
    c. colonel

____ 3. The *opposite* of **implicit** is
    a. specific
    b. perfect
    c. permanent

____ 4. The *opposite* of **adroit** is
    a. difficult
    b. graceful
    c. clumsy

____ 5. The *opposite* of **germane** is
    a. healthy
    b. inappropriate
    c. stimulating

_____ 6. **Ultimate** : final ::
   a. leader : follower
   b. mediocre : average
   c. cautious : careworn

_____ 7. **Peripheral** : edge ::
   a. shallow : deep
   b. internal : external
   c. marginal : border

_____ 8. **Formidable** : dreadful ::
   a. corrupt : horrible
   b. appalling : shocking
   c. reassuring : frightening

_____ 9. If someone is **equivocal**, then he or she is definitely *not*
   a. doubtful
   b. vague
   c. certain

_____ 10. If you feel **whimsical**, then you feel
   a. depressed
   b. impulsive
   c. watchful

Adjectives: descriptive words, *-ous* words

1. **felicitous** (fi LIS i təs)

    a. The timing of the money's arrival was so *felicitous* that Martha now believes in miracles.

    b. The veterinarian's *felicitous* words helped to comfort the little girl over the loss of her beloved dog.

2. **garrulous** (GAR ə ləs)

    a. Lois is one of the most *garrulous* persons I know; she has such a gift for talk that I think she should enter politics.

    b. Ron is not *garrulous*, but when he does have something to say, he's worth listening to.

3. **heinous** (HA nəs)

    a. Some of the scenes in the movie are so *heinous* that I would strongly urge you to avoid seeing the film.

    b. One of the most *heinous* crimes is that of child abuse.

4. **meticulous** (mə TIK yə ləs)

    a. German workers are respected throughout the word for the *meticulous* care they take in manufacturing products.

    b. Mitch took *meticulous* care of his 1957 Chevrolet, driving only in good weather and polishing it regularly.

5. **obsequious** (əb SĒ kwē əs)

    a. Carolee would do anything the boss asked; such *obsequious* behavior is disgusting.

    b. Dirk found it extremely difficult to obey and to be *obsequious* to his superiors throughout his basic training.

6. specious (SPĒ shəs)

   a. The reporter believed that the government representatives had given a *specious*, rather than an honest, response to her question.
   b. The political campaign featured a large number of *specious* arguments.

7. tenacious (tə NĀ shəs)

   a. The merger was difficult to negotiate because each party was *tenacious* in maintaining its position.
   b. Both Grant and Lee were *tenacious* Civil War generals, seldom retreating in battle despite difficulties.

8. ubiquitous (ū BIK wi təs)

   a. The *ubiquitous* puppy knocked over the wastepaper basket in the kitchen, tore down the curtains in the bedroom, and ripped open the hose in the garden.
   b. Kenna's job as a reporter required her to attend every important function in the small town, from city council meetings to high school athletic events. Soon, people in the community took her *ubiquitous* presence for granted.

9. vacuous (VAK ū əs)

   a. Don's *vacuous* comments throughout the meeting irritated me. He should learn to keep quiet when he has nothing of significance to say.
   b. Bridget struggled to find the right words to express her appreciation for the honor, but she was sure her remarks sounded *vacuous*.

10. zealous (ZEL əs)

   a. Gigi is *zealous* about her jogging; she runs at least three miles every day.
   b. Stefano, a *zealous* Lincoln scholar, is looking forward to his trip to Springfield, Illinois, where Lincoln's home and tomb are located.

EXERCISES FOR LESSON 28
Adjectives: descriptive words, -*ous* words

I. *Directions:* Match each definition to the word part it defines.

_____	**1.** felicitous	**a.** wicked, hateful
_____	**2.** garrulous	**b.** unyielding, stubborn, steadfast
_____	**3.** heinous	**c.** submissive, humbly obedient
_____	**4.** meticulous	**d.** stupid, lacking intellectual content
_____	**5.** obsequious	**e.** attractive but misleading, false
_____	**6.** specious	**f.** talkative, wordy
_____	**7.** tenacious	**g.** enthusiastic, dedicated
_____	**8.** ubiquitous	**h.** precise, particular
_____	**9.** vacuous	**i.** being everywhere, widespread
_____	**10.** zealous	**j.** appropriate, timely

II. *Directions:* In each space, write the appropriate word from those listed below.

felicitous	heinous	obsequious	tenacious	vacuous
garrulous	meticulous	specious	ubiquitous	zealous

1. The robber's _____ assault left the victim near death.

2. Because of her experience as a hospital volunteer, Brigitte was able to make _____ comments during her interview for admittance to the physical therapy program.

3. Rosemary stated that you have to be dedicated, disciplined, and _____ to succeed in the business world.

4. After the police officer stopped Karen for speeding, she made some _____ remarks about her car's speedometer not being accurate.

5. I like Otis, but he's such a _____ fellow that it's virtually impossible for me to get a word in edgewise.

6. Through the years, there have been a number of _____ reports that Elvis Presley is still alive.

7. For decades, archaeologists have conducted _____ excavations in Egypt, birthplace of one of the earliest civilizations.

8. The priest was a _____ individual, often seen visiting patients in the hospital, attending civic events, and cheering at ballgames.

9. Liz is a _____ basketball fan; she hasn't missed a home game in the past four seasons.

10. When Felix, the tough old neighborhood cat, slinks across our lawn, my collie cringes into a small ball and meekly wags his tail; such _____ behavior amuses me.

III. *Directions:* Write *Yes* in the space if the italicized word is used correctly, *No* if it is not.

_____ 1. The police chief's *felicitous* statements eventually calmed the angry crowd.

_____ 2. The old, *garrulous* apple tree produced a bountiful crop every year.

_____ 3. The topping on the delicious dessert was so *heinous* that Zelda boldly asked for another piece.

_____ 4. Dr. Waterhouse is a *meticulous* dentist, a fact that his patients appreciate.

_____ 5. My neighbor was angry and *obsequious* when my son accidentally broke one of her windows.

_____ 6. John is a *specious* friend to many people because of his thoughtfulness and dependability.

_____ 7. People describe Uncle Ben as a stubborn old man, but he considers himself as a determined and *tenacious* senior citizen.

_____ 8. Herb gave a disrespectful, *ubiquitous* answer to my polite question.

_____ 9. Numerous critics judged the play as a *vacuous* attempt to comment on the social inequities of British society.

_____ 10. Main Street shone with *zealous* neon lights.

IV. *Directions:* After selecting your response, put the letter that is before it in the space provided.

_____ 1. Which phrase would you associate with **tenacious**?
  a. holding the top cards
  b. keeping a firm hold
  c. running to keep up

_____ 2. Which word is most closely associated with **meticulous**?
  a. careful
  b. colorful
  c. curious

_____ 3. The *opposite* of **garrulous** is
  a. arguing
  b. babbling
  c. concise

_____ 4. The *opposite* of **zealous** is
  a. nonchalant
  b. affectionate
  c. industrious

_____ 5. Specious : dishonesty ::
  a. frank : truth
  b. tedious : falsehood
  c. specific : deception

_____ 6. Felicitous : unfortunate
  a. alike : different
  b. timely : lucky
  c. graceful : skillful

_____ 7. Vacuous : empty ::
  a. vacancy : filled
  b. vague : distinct
  c. void : unoccupied

_____ 8. Heinous : hideous ::
  a. monstrous : alluring
  b. attractive : charming
  c. beautiful : repulsive

_____ **9. Ubiquitous** : worldwide
   a. existing : regional
   b. exclusive : national
   c. everywhere : universal

_____ **10.** Which person would you associate with **obsequious**?
   a. self-seeking flatterer
   b. insensitive administrator
   c. arrogant movie star

Adjectives: descriptive words, *-ous* words

1. **acrimonious** (ak rə MO nē əs)

   a. Nathan thought that Sue and Leonard were having an *acrimonious* discussion, but he later learned that they had only been kidding each other.
   b. The *acrimonious* shouting between the two small boys started when one boy made fun of the other's dog.

2. **ambiguous** (am BIG ū əs)

   a. Presidents sometimes give *ambiguous* answers at press conferences because direct responses to sensitive questions would jeopardize national security.
   b. Although Mike was eager to see his relatives in Minnesota again, he was *ambiguous* about flying because he had suffered from motion sickness on a previous flight.

3. **gregarious** (gri GAR ē əs)

   a. Wendell had a difficult time adjusting to college the first semester, mostly because he is not *gregarious* with strangers.
   b. Lila is so thoughtful and *gregarious* that everyone likes her.

4. **indigenous** (in DIJ ə nəs)

   a. Evergreen trees, such as spruce and pine, are *indigenous* to New Hampshire.
   b. Are kangaroos *indigenous* only to Australia?

5. **magnanimous** (mag NAN ə məs)

   a. Yusef is such a *magnanimous* person that he didn't even mention that I was responsible for his painful injury.
   b. Abraham Lincoln displayed a compassionate, *magnanimous* spirit toward friend and foe alike.

6. **ominous** (OM ə nəs)

    a. Mr. Butler decided to postpone his trip to St. Louis because the winter sky looked *ominous*.

    b. The coach didn't believe he would lose his job despite *ominous* mutterings from alumni and sportswriters.

7. **pompous** (POM pəs)

    a. Max initially believed that the new district attorney was a rather *pompous* person, but he discovered that she was actually quite friendly and down-to-earth.

    b. After Jackie inherited a fortune, she acted *pompous* for a time, but she eventually realized she would have no friends left if she continued her stuck-up ways.

8. **spurious** (SPYOOR ē əs)

    a. The judge sternly lectured the witness for giving *spurious* testimony; he pointed out that there are severe penalties for lying under oath.

    b. Banks in the metropolitan area were alerted after *spurious* twenty-dollar bills began turning up in a number of nearby malls.

9. **vicarious** (vi KAR ē əs)

    a. Some people who would love to travel have to be content with the *vicarious* experience of reading *National Geographic* magazines.

    b. Because her landlord will not permit her to have a dog in her apartment, Charlene has to settle for the *vicarious* satisfaction she derives from visiting some friends who own a beautiful collie.

10. **voracious** (vō RĀ shəs)

    a. My dog has a *voracious* appetite; he consumes any food in sight.

    b. Juan, who loves to learn, is a *voracious* reader.

EXERCISES FOR LESSON 29
Adjectives: descriptive words, *-ous* words

I. *Directions:* Match each definition to the word part it defines.

_____ 1. acrimonious   a. uncertain, unclear, indefinite

_____ 2. ambiguous   b. snobbish, arrogant, egotistical

_____ 3. gregarious   c. substituting one experience for that of another

_____ 4. indigenous   d. threatening, disturbing

_____ 5. magnanimous   e. sarcastic, bitter in speech or behavior

_____ 6. ominous   f. native to a particular region, natural, inborn

_____ 7. pompous   g. high-minded, demonstrating generosity of spirit, noble

_____ 8. spurious   h. greedy in eating, incapable of being satisfied

_____ 9. vicarious   i. false, phony

_____ 10. voracious   j. sociable, enjoying the company of others

II. *Directions:* In each space, write the appropriate word from those listed below.

| acrimonious | gregarious | magnanimous | pompous | vicarious |
| ambiguous | indigenous | ominous | spurious | voracious |

1. People of all faiths demonstrated a _____ spirit by donating money and time to help rebuild the historic church.

2. My brother has a _____ appetite for Mexican food.

3. The inheritance will go to the proper person once it has been established which will is authentic and which one is _____.

4. The _____ feelings that exist between the two neighbors were originally caused by a boundary dispute.

5. Rubber trees are not _____ to any region of the United States.

6. Some of the citizens in the small town obviously resented those college students who behaved in a superior, _____ manner.

7. Because customers appreciate Gino's humor and _____ behavior, he is the most popular waiter at the restaurant.

8. The crowd seemed to be getting a _____ thrill just by watching others ride the rollercoaster.

9. In the old Western movie I was watching on television, the bad guy in the black hat made some _____ threats to the rancher who refused to sell his land to him.

10. Many young people have _____ feelings when they graduate from high school; they are happy to have accomplished such a major goal, but, on the other hand, they are sad to have completed this part of their lives.

III. *Directions:* Write *Yes* in the space if the italicized word is used correctly, *No* if it is not.

_____ 1. Despite the intensity of the game, none of the players displayed *acrimonious* behavior toward one another.

_____ 2. Because she's not feeling too well, Vicki is somewhat *ambiguous* about attending the concert.

_____ 3. Kentucky, with its *gregarious* pastures and handsome horse farms, is a beautiful state.

_____ 4. Mona suffered from an *indigenous* stomach after drinking two glasses of wine and eating a pint of oysters.

_____ 5. The *magnanimous* car had every accessory that you can imagine.

_____ 6. When the driver began to protest his speeding ticket, the state trooper gave him an *ominous* look.

_____ 7. Jake's elbow was still swollen and *pompous*, but he said it felt much better.

_____ 8. The rain came fast and *spurious*, so the crops were saved.

_____ 9. Dr. Domani got a *vicarious* thrill out of seeing the children that she had delivered grow up to be successful.

_____ 10. I don't understand how my friends can afford such a large, *voracious* house in the suburbs.

IV. *Directions:* After selecting your response, put the letter that is before it in the space provided.

_____ 1. **Spurious** suggests
   a. commitment
   b. deception
   c. unconcern

_____ 2. **Gregarious** suggests
   a. treachery
   b. friendliness
   c. isolation

_____ 3. Which of these animals are **indigenous** to Florida?
   a. alligators
   b. kangaroos
   c. elephants

_____ 4. The *opposite* of **magnanimous** is
   a. generous
   b. selfish
   c. puzzling

_____ 5. **Ominous** : evil ::
   a. unlucky : disaster
   b. promising : profit
   c. threatening : wickedness

_____ 6. **Acrimonious** : friendly ::
   a. friendly : cordial
   b. cordial : aloof
   c. aloof : withdrawn

_____ 7. **Voracious** : moderate ::
   a. extreme : farthest
   b. restrict : curb
   c. tolerant : impatient

_____ 8. **Ambiguous**: definite ::
   a. doubtful : certain
   b. hesitant : slow
   c. extravagant : exaggeration

_____ 9. If a person is **pompous**, then he or she is certainly *not*
   a. honest
   b. proud
   c. humble

_____ 10. A **vicarious** experience is
   a. second-best
   b. second-class
   c. second-hand

Adjectives: descriptive words, *-ous* words

1. **arduous** (AR jū əs)

   a. The survivors made the *arduous* hike over the mountain.
   b. Gustav knows from experience that baling hay in Iowa's summer heat is *arduous* work.

2. **autonomous** (ə TON ə məs)

   a. The Philippines, once under the guardianship of the United States, has been an *autonomous* nation since 1946.
   b. Jan is not interested in forming a partnership as he much prefers operating on an *autonomous* basis.

3. **chivalrous** (SHIV əl rəs)

   a. Hugo's *chivalrous* manners may be out of style, but I appreciate them.
   b. I appreciated the *chivalrous* way in which Elliott accepted responsibility for the project's failure.

4. **copious** (KŌ pē əs)

   a. Mavis lost a *copious* amount of blood when her nose was broken in a bicycle accident.
   b. Police investigations involve *copious* records and reports.

5. **deleterious** (del i TĒR ē əs)

   a. Felicia's inattention in her political science class had a *deleterious* effect when it came time to take her midterm exam.
   b. Some psychologists maintain that unrestricted television viewing can have *deleterious* influences on children.

6. **diaphanous** (dī AF ə nəs)

   a. Sheer, clear nylon is one type of material used to make *diaphanous* garments.
   b. Polly was obviously self-conscious in her flimsy, *diaphanous* dress, but she looked very attractive.

7. **incongruous** (in KONG groo əs)

   a. It seems *incongruous* to me that Judy, who never goes out of her way to make friends, is often the person others turn to for advice.
   b. Reggie's friends find it *incongruous* that he's enrolled in a premed program when they know he can't stand the sight of blood.

8. **ludicrous** (LOO də krəs)

   a. It's *ludicrous* the way some people baby their pets.
   b. The master of ceremonies tried to be funny when he introduced each act, but I thought his comments were *ludicrous*.

9. **nebulous** (NEB yə ləs)

   a. Terri's plans are still in the *nebulous* stage, but she hopes to have the time and money to do some traveling.
   b. Sooner or later *nebulous* ideas must be translated into positive action if we are to succeed.

10. **vociferous** (vō SIF ər əs)

    a. Hockey fans have the reputation for being the rowdiest, most *vociferous* of all sports fans.
    b. The city council had heard *vociferous* complaints because of the increase in property taxes.

EXERCISES FOR LESSON 30
Adjectives: descriptive words, *-ous* words

I. *Directions:* Match each definition to the word part it defines.

_____	**1.** arduous	**a.** transparent, delicate, letting light through
_____	**2.** autonomous	**b.** abundant, great quantity, large number
_____	**3.** chivalrous	**c.** inappropriate, illogical
_____	**4.** copious	**d.** difficult, involving great hardship
_____	**5.** deleterious	**e.** hazy, indistinct, vague
_____	**6.** diaphanous	**f.** gallant, courteous, self-sacrificing
_____	**7.** incongruous	**g.** loudly vocal, howling, boisterous
_____	**8.** ludicrous	**h.** harmful, injurious, destructive
_____	**9.** nebulous	**i.** self-governing, independent
_____	**10.** vociferous	**j.** ridiculous, absurd, foolish

II. *Directions:* In each space, write the appropriate word from those listed below.

arduous   chivalrous   deleterious   incongruous   nebulous
autonomous copious   diaphanous   ludicrous   vociferous

1. Many football jerseys are now made of light, _____ material.

2. A spokeswoman for the environmental group made an angry, _____ speech to the newspaper reporters when she learned that the off-shore drilling would be allowed to continue.

3. Wearing oversized shoes and a loose-fitting suit, the young man looked quite _____.

4. Mr. Pierce's office is filled with _____ mementos, ranging from dozens of photographs to scores of framed citations from various civic organizations.

5. Roberto finds it _____ that his wife, who obviously loves her parents, refuses to invite them for a meal.

6. Despite the injustice of the accusations, Daryl kept her poise and behaved in a _____ manner.

7. If that movie has a message, then it's too _____ for me to figure out.

8. Jesse spent an _____ summer on a cattle ranch, working constantly from sunrise to sunset.

9. Priscilla knew that dwelling on her disappointment was having a _____ effect on her morale, so she vowed to forget it.

10. Scotland is part of the United Kingdom; it is not an _____ country.

III. *Directions:* Write *Yes* in the space if the italicized word is used correctly, *No* if it is not.

_____ **1.** Tim was finding paratroop training as *arduous* as his friends told him it would be.

_____ **2.** The rain came just in time to help the *autonomous* corn crop.

_____ **3.** Nolan became *chivalrous* from the cold, bitter wind.

_____ **4.** Eventually, we will have to master the *copious* details in the computer manual.

_____ **5.** The audience became *deleterious* from the comic's antics and jokes.

_____ **6.** My husband and I decided it was time to buy a *diaphanous* washing machine.

_____ **7.** With condominiums and high-rise apartment buildings all around, it was *incongruous* to find an old farmhouse.

_____ **8.** Rita was embarrassed by her little brother's *ludicrous* behavior when her friends came by to study.

_____ **9.** Joanne looked at the *nebulous* figure on the ultrasound screen and found it difficult to believe that in a few short weeks a human life would be easily recognizable.

_____ **10.** Gene made a *vociferous* complaint to his supervisor when he was transferred to the midnight shift.

IV. *Directions:* After selecting your response, put the letter that is before it in the space provided.

_____ 1. Which word is related to **ludicrous**?
    a. foolishness
    b. smoothness
    c. vividness

_____ 2. Which of the following is most likely to be **diaphanous**?
    a. accordion
    b. blouse
    c. carpet

_____ 3. Which word is associated with **vociferous**?
    a. inactivity
    b. insecurity
    c. intensity

_____ 4. A **chivalrous** person is certainly *not*
    a. happy
    b. discourteous
    c. confused

_____ 5. **Copious** : scarce ::
    a. quality : quantity
    b. plenty : abundant
    c. common : rare

_____ 6. **Nebulous** : cloudy ::
    a. hazy : fuzzy
    b. dark : pale
    c. distinct : transparent

_____ 7. **Arduous** : easy ::
    a. tiring : fatiguing
    b. difficult : simple
    c. large : enormous

_____ 8. **Autonomous** : free ::
    a. free : independent
    b. independent : reliance
    c. reliance : liberty

_____ **9. Incongruous** suggests
   a. astonishment
   b. disloyalty
   c. scandal

_____ **10. Deleterious** suggests
   a. success
   b. preparation
   c. ruin

Academic Terms

Section Three presents you with an opportunity to become familiar with many of the academic terms associated with subjects you are likely to study in college, including literature, composition, psychology, sociology, history, political science, business, economics, music, art, biology, chemistry, physics, astronomy, and computer science. Appendix C also includes the definitions of word parts helpful to your understanding of numerous biological and physical science terms.

You will notice that some words from our everyday conversation are limited to a precise meaning when they are used as academic terms. Your knowledge of these meanings is essential because they are among those that you must clearly understand to grasp important basic concepts in the various courses.

The following lessons provide definitions similar to what you would find in the glossary of a textbook. Further, they present a sentence demonstrating the word's appropriate use. Some words contain parts that you have studied; these word parts are underlined for easy recognition. Begin each lesson by carefully studying these definitions, sentences, and word parts; then complete the exercises. Have your work checked after each lesson, and be prepared for a mastery test after you have studied all the terms for each subject.

Literature and Composition

Literature and composition embrace all human experiences—common, unique, sad, joyful, expected, unexpected, disenchanting, and inspirational. These subjects can provide excellent opportunities to gain valuable insights into life. The following terms are commonly used in both literature and composition, so knowledge of them will be beneficial to you.

1. **prose** (PRŌZ)—noun
   The ordinary form of language; that is, writing or speech that is not poetry.
   Novels and short stories are almost always written in *prose*.

2. **genre** (ZHAN rə)—noun
   A category or type of literature, such as novels, autobiography, or short story.
   Biography, an account of a person's life, is the most popular *genre* of literature for many readers.

3. **bibliography** (bib lē OG rə fē)—noun
   A list of books and other readings on a particular subject.
   A research paper's *bibliography* must list all the sources used for information.

4. **denotation** (dē nō TĀ shən)—noun
   The strict, exact meaning of a word.
   The *denotation* of "father" is "male parent."

5. **connotation** (kon ə TĀ shən)—noun
   A word's suggested meanings or emotional associations, as contrasted to its strict, exact meaning.
   The denotation of "home" is "residence," but the *connotation* of "home" suggests feelings of love and security.

6. **literal** (LIT ər əl)—adjective
   Literal, as is true of *denotation*, refers to the strict meaning of a word or phrase.
   The *literal* meaning of "mother" is "female parent."

189

7. **figures of speech**—noun

Expressions in which the words are not meant in their literal sense but are intended to be interpreted in an imaginative way.

To present information in an original and a colorful manner, writers often use *figures of speech*.

8. **simile** (SIM ə lē)—noun

A figure of speech in which two unlike things are compared by using the words *like* or *as*.

"The frisky puppy is like an unguided missile" is an example of a *simile*.

9. **metaphor** (MET ə for)—noun

A figure of speech in which two unlike things are compared or one thing is said to be another thing; the words *like* or *as* are not used in the comparison.

"On Saturday evenings, Whitney's car was a panther that slinked down Main Street daring anyone or anything to challenge it" is an example of a *metaphor*.

10. **personification** (pər son ə fa KĀ shən)—noun

A figure of speech in which a nonhuman thing is given human qualities or performs human actions.

"The tulips danced and smiled when the old gardener came their way" is an example of *personification*.

EXERCISES FOR LESSON 31
Literature and Composition

I. *Directions:* Match each definition with the word it defines.

_____ **1.** prose   **a.** imaginative expressions

_____ **2.** genre   **b.** adjective referring to the exact meaning of a word or phrase

_____ **3.** bibliography   **c.** noun referring to the actual meaning

_____ **4.** denotation   **d.** giving a nonhuman thing human qualities

_____ **5.** connotation   **e.** writing that is not poetry

_____ **6.** literal   **f.** suggested meaning of a word

_____ **7.** figures of speech   **g.** list of readings or references

_____ **8.** simile   **h.** comparison using *like* or *as*

_____ **9.** metaphor   **i.** form of literature

_____ **10.** personification   **j.** comparison not using *like* or *as*

II. *Directions:* In each space, write the appropriate word or words from those listed below.

bibliography	denotation	genre	metaphor	prose
connotation	figures of speech	literal	personification	simile

1. "Grover's motorboat is like a rocket" is a _____.

2. "Diego was a perfectly tuned machine; he ran relentlessly mile after mile" is a _____.

3. Personification, metaphors, and similes are _____.

4. Most magazines are written in _____.

5. At the end of your term paper, include a _____ containing all the references you have used.

6. The _____ of the word "football" includes fall afternoons, marching bands, and roaring crowds.

7. The _____ of the word "football" includes a game played by eleven players on each team.

8. Poetry is another _____ of literature.

9. "The tree stuck out its leg and tripped me" is _____.

10. The _____ meaning of "morning" is the time between 12:00 A.M. and 12:00 P.M.

III. *Directions:* If the words opposite each other in Columns A and B are similar in meaning, write *Yes* in the blank; if they are unrelated, write *No.*

A	B
1. prose	____ rhyming words
2. genre	____ family history
3. bibliography	____ list of readings
4. denotation	____ word's actual meaning
5. connotation	____ word's opposite meaning
6. literal	____ reading ability
7. figures of speech	____ fanciful expressions
8. simile	____ comparison without *like* or *as*
9. metaphor	____ comparison with *like* or *as*
10. personification	____ sociable

IV. *Directions:* Write either an original sentence or a definition for each word that clearly demonstrates your mastery of its meaning as used in literature and composition.

1. prose _____

_____

2. genre _____

_____

3. bliography _____

_____

4. denotation _____

_____

5. connotation _____

_____

6. literal _____

_____

7. figures of speech _____

_____

8. simile _____

_____

9. metaphor _____

_____

10. personification _____

_____

Literature and Composition

1. **hyper<u>bole</u>** (hī PUR bə lē)—noun
Figurative language in which exaggerated words are used for emphasis.
"The closet in my room is so small that an ant wouldn't have enough room to turn around" is an example of *hyperbole*.

2. **allitera<u>tion</u>** (ə lit ə RĀ shən)—noun
Alliteration is the repetition of the first sound in a series of words.
"Francis is fair, frank, friendly, and famous" is an example of *alliteration*.

3. **plagiar<u>ism</u>** (PLĀ jə riz əm)—noun
Plagiarism is the copying of words or ideas of another writer and the presenting of them as one's original work.
You must give credit to the author of the words you are using; otherwise, you will be guilty of *plagiarism*.

4. **satire** (SAT īr)—noun
The use of sarcastic humor to expose injustices or stupidity.
The sports columnist's *satire* was obvious when she wrote that the owner of the basketball team should feel guilty for not giving his star player a house since the player was making "only" $950,000 a year.

5. **tone** (TŌN)—noun
A writer's basic attitude or point of view toward a subject, such as serious, humorous, romantic, impersonal.
Peter Jenkins uses a personal *tone* in his book *Walk Across America*.

6. **prewriting** (prē RĪ ting)—noun

A vital stage of the writing process in which writers attempt to bring their ideas into focus. To stimulate their thinking about topics, writers use prewriting techniques such as the following: asking themselves basic questions about a topic; writing rapidly and nonstop about anything that comes to mind about a topic; making a list of details about a topic.

Christine says that the most helpful *prewriting* activity for her is simply to jot down for twenty minutes or so anything that pops into her mind about a subject.

7. **narration** (na RĀ shən)—noun

A type of writing that relates a story or series of events, which can be either true or fictional.

In my composition class, the first assignment in *narration* required us to write about a frightening event that we had experienced.

8. **exposition** (ek spə ZISH ən)—noun

A type of nonfiction writing that explains or informs.

Our first assignment in *exposition* was to explain why we had chosen to attend a military academy.

9. **description** (di SKRIP shən)—noun

A type of writing that presents vivid sense details for the purpose of conveying a mood or presenting information about how something looks, feels, tastes, sounds, smells, or works.

Our first writing assignment in *description* was to present vivid details about the main street in our hometown.

10. **argumentation** (ar gū men TĀ shən)—noun

A type of writing that attempts to persuade the reader to a particular point of view about a subject. Along with narration, exposition, and description, argumentation is one of the major forms of writing.

Our first writing assignment in *argumentation* was to research Maine's recently proposed drunk-driving bill, then to argue either for or against its passage.

EXERCISES FOR LESSON 32
Literature and Composition

I. *Directions:* Match each definition with the word it defines.

_____ **1.** hyperbole   **a.** sarcastic and mocking humor that exposes vice or stupidity

_____ **2.** alliteration   **b.** writing that tells a story

_____ **3.** plagiarism   **c.** author's point of view about a topic

_____ **4.** satire   **d.** writing devoted to sense impressions

_____ **5.** tone   **e.** writing that tries to convince

_____ **6.** prewriting   **f.** a string of words with the same initial sound

_____ **7.** narration   **g.** step in writing involving the forming of ideas

_____ **8.** exposition   **h.** exaggeration for the sake of effect

_____ **9.** description   **i.** writing that instructs or clarifies

_____ **10.** argumentation   **j.** representing the words or ideas of another author as one's own

II. *Directions:* In each space, write the appropriate word from those listed below.

alliteration	description	hyperbole	plagiarism	satire
argumentation	exposition	narration	prewriting	tone

1. "Bruce brutally batted ball after ball" is an example of _____.

2. Gerard's major _____ in his paper is of regret.

3. An editorial devoted to reasons why a senior citizens' center should be built would be writing of _____.

4. Before trying to do any actual writing, Roger tape-recorded his random thoughts about the topic. This activity was part of Roger's _____.

5. "I drove a million miles during my week's vacation" is obviously

_____.

6. If I want you to experience what my old high school gym looked like, I must do the type of writing called _____.

7. Max didn't want to commit _____, so he put quotation marks around the words and mentioned the author's name.

8. Juanita's paper was about the specific procedures to follow in parachute jumping; her writing, therefore, was mainly

_____.

9. In his letter to the editor, Mr. Belson used bitter humor, or _____, to voice his criticisms about the new fishing regulations.

10. Marilyn's paper is a funny account of her adventures while scuba diving off the southern coast of Florida; her paper, therefore, was mainly

_____.

III. *Directions:* If the words opposite each other in Columns A and B are similar in meaning, write *Yes* in the blank; if they are unrelated, write *No.*

A		B
1. hyperbole	____	factual information
2. alliteration	____	series of words with the same first sound
3. plagiarism	____	summarizing a play
4. satire	____	concluding remarks
5. tone	____	point of view
6. prewriting	____	final written version
7. narration	____	writing that tells a story
8. exposition	____	writing emphasizing explanations
9. description	____	writing emphasizing precise details
10. argumentation	____	writing that attempts to persuade

IV. *Directions:* Write either an original sentence or a definition for each word that clearly demonstrates your mastery of its meaning as used in literature and composition.

1. **hyperbole** _____

_____

2. **alliteration** _____

_____

3. **plagiarism** _____

_____

4. **satire** _____

_____

5. **tone** _____

_____

6. **prewriting** _____

_____

7. **narration** _____

_____

8. **exposition** _____

_____

9. **description** _____

_____

10. argumentation _____

_____

TAKE THE WORD MASTERY TEST FOR LITERATURE AND COMPOSITION.

Psychology

Psychology is devoted to the systematic study of behavior as well as to the motives for that behavior. Mastery of the following psychological terms can contribute to your understanding of this interesting subject.

1. **organism** (OR gə niz əm)—noun
   Any living animal or plant.
   A monkey was injected with the *organism* for the experiment.

2. **motor skills** (MŌ tər SKILS)—noun
   A coordinated series of physical movements, such as those required to walk or swim.
   Gymnastics requires advanced development of many *motor skills*.

3. **theory** (THĒR ē)—noun
   An association of ideas that attempts to provide a reasonable explanation for events observed or to predict what will be observed under a given set of circumstances.
   One *theory* is that the moon was once part of the earth.

4. **cognitive** (KOG nət iv)—adjective
   Relating to knowing, understanding, thinking.
   A major stage in a child's *cognitive* development is reached when he or she becomes capable of abstract reasoning.

5. **behavior** (bi HĀV yər)—noun
   Any activity of a human or other organism.
   Thinking, though unobservable, is part of a person's *behavior*.

6. **variable** (VAR ē ə bəl)—noun
   In an experiment, a variable is the condition or factor that can be changed or manipulated.
   The brand of tires was the only *variable* involved in the testing of the car's gas-mileage performances.

7. **empirical** (em PIR ə kəl)—adjective
   Relating to what has been precisely experienced or observed in experiments.
   The *empirical* facts were recorded so that the experiment could be evaluated.

8. **experimental group**—noun
   A group of subjects, which could be people or other organisms, exposed to the variable being investigated in an experiment. The researcher is attempting to discover the effects of the variable.
   Both groups were on the same diet; however, only the *experimental group* was led in exercises for fifteen minutes a day. This was to determine whether or not exercises of that duration would contribute to additional weight loss.

9. **control group**—noun
   A group of subjects exposed to all the features of a particular experiment except for the variable being studied. The characteristics of the control group are always matched as closely as possible to those of the experimental group.
   The experimental group, which was given the vaccine, had significantly fewer colds and other viruses during the twelve weeks of the investigation than did the *control group*, which was not administered the vaccine.

10. **sibling** (SIB ling)—adjective
    One of two or more individuals having one common parent; usually a brother or a sister.
    A case of *sibling* rivalry exists between Jack and his brother; they are obviously jealous of each other's success.

EXERCISES FOR LESSON 33
Psychology

I. *Directions:* Match each definition with the word it defines.

_____ 1. organism

a. based upon observable facts or experiences

_____ 2. motor skills

b. relating to knowing and thinking

_____ 3. theory

c. a brother or sister

_____ 4. cognitive

d. condition manipulated in an experiment

_____ 5. behavior

e. a living creature

_____ 6. variable

f. those in an experiment exposed to the treatment condition

_____ 7. empirical

g. reasonable explanation

_____ 8. experimental group

h. any activity of an organism

_____ 9. control group

i. physical abilities that involve movement

_____ 10. sibling

j. those in an experiment not exposed to the treatment condition

II. *Directions:* In each space, write the appropriate word or words from those listed below.

behavior   motor skills
cognitive   organism
control group   sibling
empirical   theory
experimental group   variable

1. Bradley believes he has the necessary _____ to do a somersault on skis.

2. Dr. Skolberg's _____ is that vitamin C's ability to prevent colds and other viral infections has been greatly exaggerated.

3. Marguerite was a member of the _____, so she received vitamin C.

4. Kristin, however, was a member of the _____, so she did not receive vitamin C.

5. Thus, vitamin C was the _____ manipulated in this experiment.

6. Based upon the _____ evidence, Dr. Clarke concluded that vitamin C was somewhat helpful in the prevention of colds and other viral infections.

7. Is Todd's oldest _____ a brother or a sister?

8. A guinea pig was the subject, or _____, used by the fourth grade class in its nutritional study.

9. The psychological definition of _____ includes all activities, both physical and mental, done by a person or other organism.

10. As a person matures, his or her _____ skills become more developed, so he or she is capable of solving more complex problems.

III. *Directions:* If the words opposite each other in Columns A and B are similar in meaning, write *Yes* in the blank; if they are unrelated, write *No*.

A		B
1. organism	____	living creature
2. motor skills	____	physical abilities
3. theory	____	truth
4. cognitive	____	classification
5. behavior	____	all activities
6. variable	____	disagreement
7. empirical	____	costly
8. experimental group	____	those exposed to the factor manipulated in an experiment
9. control group	____	those not included in an experiment
10. sibling	____	mother or father

IV. *Directions:* Write either an original sentence or a definition for each word that clearly demonstrates your mastery of its meaning as used in psychology.

1. **organism** _____

_____

2. **motor skills** _____

_____

3. **theory** _____

_____

4. **cognitive** _____

_____

5. **behavior** _____

_____

6. **variable** _____

_____

7. **empirical** _____

_____

8. **experimental group** _____

_____

9. **control group** _____

_____

10. **sibling** _____

_____

Psychology

1. **defense mechanisms**—noun
   Unconscious strategies for protecting ourselves against unpleasant emotions and anxiety.
   Repression, or selective forgetting, is a common *defense mechanism*.

2. **rationalization** (rash nə lə ZĀ shən)—noun
   A common defense mechanism in which people justify their disappointing behavior or situation by devising excuses to explain it instead of admitting the actual reasons.
   When Earl did not receive the raise he had requested, his *rationalization* was that he didn't really care anyway, since state and federal taxes would have taken most of the raise.

3. **repression** (rə PRESH ən)—noun
   A common defense mechanism in which upsetting motives, conflicts, or emotions are pushed from the conscious to the unconscious level.
   As a result of *repression*, Del didn't realize that the reason he no longer visited his uncle's home was that it was associated with the death of his favorite cousin.

4. **intrinsic motivation** (in TRIN sik)—noun
   A reason or desire for action that comes from within the individual.
   Carolyn wants to prove to herself that she can get better grades, so her additional studying is the result of *intrinsic motivation*.

5. **extrinsic motivation** (eks TRIN sik)—noun
   A reason or desire for action that comes from outside the individual.
   Matthew's increased studying this semester results from *extrinsic motivation*—his folks promised him $400 if he improved all his grades.

6. **conditioning** (kən DISH ə ning)—noun
Training that results in the subject's learning a particular response to a particular stimulus.
Mrs. Bryson's dog has learned through *conditioning* to stand quietly but alertly at the front door every time the doorbell rings.

7. **therapeutic** (ther ə PŪ tik)—adjective
Relating to the treatment of disease, especially describing something intended to bring about healing.
Kara says that playing her clarinet has a *therapeutic* effect on her when she is worried.

8. **free association**—noun
A therapeutic method in which the patient is encouraged to talk in an unrestricted manner in the belief that this approach may lead to the discovery of repressed conflicts.
Because the doctor is convinced that *free association* uncovers hidden conflicts, the patient has been encouraged to talk without censorship about any topic that comes to mind.

9. **behavior therapy**—noun
Behavior therapy is a direct approach that concentrates on helping patients learn more appropriate ways of acting and thinking to overcome their problems. It is concerned with changing a person's behavior.
The psychologist used *behavior therapy* to help the patient overcome a fear of crowds by gradually increasing the number of people with whom the patient was in contact.

10. **paranoia** (par ə NOI ə)—noun
A mental illness characterized by delusions of grandeur and persecution.
The patient, who says he is the world's foremost authority on military strategy, believes that numerous foreign agents are attempting to kill him; he has been a victim of this *paranoia* since he was in his late teens.

EXERCISES FOR LESSON 34
Psychology

I. *Directions:* Match each definition with the word it defines.

_____ **1.** defense mechanisms

    a. learning a specific response to a specific stimulus or situation

_____ **2.** rationalization

    b. discussing whatever comes to mind

_____ **3.** repression

    c. stimulation that comes from within a person

_____ **4.** intrinsic motivation

    d. unconscious devices used to reduce anxiety

_____ **5.** extrinsic motivation

    e. mental disorder marked by feelings of persecution and grandeur

_____ **6.** conditioning

    f. stimulation that comes from outside the person

_____ **7.** therapeutic

    g. descriptive term used for the treatment of illness

_____ **8.** free association

    h. when disturbing thoughts are submerged to the unconscious; selective forgetting

_____ **9.** behavior therapy

    i. treatment that teaches a patient new ways of thinking and acting

_____ **10.** paranoia

    j. the attempt to explain away failure so as to protect self-esteem

II. *Directions:* In each space, write the appropriate word or words from those listed below.

behavior therapy   intrinsic motivation
conditioning   paranoia
defense mechanisms   rationalization
extrinsic motivation   repression
free association   therapeutic

1. Rather than searching the patient's mind for hidden conflicts, _____ concentrates on teaching the individual direct ways of resolving his or her problem.

2. Molly is practicing the piano for two hours daily because of _____; her parents promised her a Florida vacation if she practiced regularly for six months.

3. People use numerous _____ to cope with disappointment as well as to protect their self-image.

4. The general term used for the teaching of a specific response to a specific stimulus is _____.

5. If a person performs some behavior because of personal reasons, he or she is prompted by _____.

6. To free your mind from everyday concerns you will find a walk in the woods to be _____.

7. On the other hand, _____ can be an effective way of uncovering deeply buried problems; that is, talking openly about any thought that comes to mind can sometimes lead to valuable insights.

8. The patient had unknowingly resorted to _____ to block out the memory of his tragic war experience.

9. The patient appeared to be suffering from _____; she was convinced that a conspiracy was responsible for her failure to be recognized as a great artist.

10. After being turned down for flight training, Kenneth said that being a pilot was probably boring anyway; his statement represents a possible _____.

III. *Directions:* If the words opposite each other in Columns A and B are similar in meaning, write *Yes* in the blank; if they are unrelated, write *No.*

A		**B**
1. defense mechanisms	____	electrical devices
2. rationalization	____	limited process
3. repression	____	burying unpleasantness
4. intrinsic motivation	____	motivation from within
5. extrinsic motivation	____	motivation from outside
6. conditioning	____	vigorous exertion
7. therapeutic	____	helpful to healing
8. free association	____	letting the mind roam
9. behavior therapy	____	harsh punishment
10. paranoia	____	delusions of persecution, grandeur

IV. *Definitions:* Write either an original sentence or a definition for each word that clearly demonstrates your mastery of its meaning as used in psychology.

1. **defense mechanisms** _____

_____

2. **rationalization** _____

_____

3. **repression** _____

_____

4. **intrinsic motivation** _____

_____

5. **extrinsic motivation** _____

_____

6. conditioning _____

   _____

7. therapeutic _____

   _____

8. free association _____

   _____

9. behavior therapy _____

   _____

10. paranoia _____

   _____

TAKE THE WORD MASTERY TEST FOR PSYCHOLOGY.

Sociology

Sociology is concerned with the systematic study of human society, including the social interactions among nations, communities, and families. Mastery of the following sociology terms can contribute to your insight into this valuable social science.

1. **social norms—noun**
   Social norms are standards that guide people in what they should or should not do in any particular social situation.
   Laws are serious and formal *social norms*.

2. **mores** (MŌR āz)**—noun**
   Mores are social norms that reflect the moral standards of a society.
   Marrying a close relative is opposed by the *mores* of all societies.

3. **values—noun**
   Values are ideas about what is good, proper, wise, and worthwhile.
   Achieving success in work is one of society's *values*.

4. **culture—noun**
   Culture is the patterns of life shared by the members of a society; these patterns are transmitted from one generation to another.
   Eating three meals a day is part of our *culture*.

5. **peer group—noun**
   A peer group is a grouping of individuals of the same general age and social position.
   As a child becomes older, his or her *peer group* has more influence.

6. **stereotype** (STER ē ə tīp)**—noun**
   A standardized image applied to individuals who are identified with a particular group.
   The *stereotype* of the cowboy of the Old West is that of a fearless, rugged, independent man.

7. **demography** (di MOG rə fē)—noun
Demography is the statistical study of human population, such as information about the number of births, deaths, and marriages.
A study of *demography* reveals that one of the highest birthrates in the United States occurred in the late 1940s.

8. **acculturation** (ə kul chə RĀ shən)—noun
Acculturation is the process of acquiring the patterns of life of a different group or society.
In Japan, *acculturation* of many aspects of Western culture began after World War II.

9. **urbanism** (UR bə niz əm)—noun
Urbanism relates to patterns of life characteristic of cities.
Some of the benefits of *urbanism* include access to outstanding museums, theaters, and restaurants.

10. **agrarian** (ə GRAR ē ən)—adjective
Agrarian relates to rural life, agricultural groups, and farm ownership.
The United States has moved from a predominantly *agrarian* to an urban society.

EXERCISES FOR LESSON 35
Sociology

I. *Directions:* Match each definition with the word it defines.

_____	**1.** social norms	**a.** adopting new patterns of life
_____	**2.** mores	**b.** a fixed view of individuals
_____	**3.** values	**c.** customs and values shared by a society
_____	**4.** culture	**d.** standards for social behavior
_____	**5.** peer group	**e.** refers to country life and farming
_____	**6.** stereotype	**f.** guides that provide moral standards
_____	**7.** demography	**g.** study of population figures
_____	**8.** acculturation	**h.** ideas about what is beneficial
_____	**9.** urbanism	**i.** refers to cities
_____	**10.** agrarian	**j.** individuals of similar backgrounds

II. *Directions:* In each space, write the appropriate word or words from those listed below.

acculturation	peer group
agrarian	social norms
culture	stereotype
demography	urbanism
mores	values

1. A word referring to city life is _____.

2. Guides that help us to decide how we should behave in public are _____.

3. Because friends are important to all of us, we wish to be accepted by our _____.

4. Human population figures have to do with the subject of _____.

5. Strict guides concerned with society's important moral standards are called _____.

6. Getting a good education is one of the _____ of our society because of education's personal and vocational benefits.

7. A person who is overly aggressive, loud, and deceptive is the _____ many people have of a used-car salesman.

8. Iowa and Nebraska are considered _____ states because of the importance of agriculture to their economy.

9. Laws, religion, and manners are part of our _____.

10. A United States citizen who moves to the Philippines undergoes an _____ process because of the necessity to acquire new ways of functioning in a different society.

III. *Directions:* If the words opposite each other in Columns A and B are similar in meaning, write *Yes* in the blank; if they are unrelated, write *No.*

A		B
1. social norms	____	behavior guides
2. mores	____	moral guidelines
3. values	____	ideals
4. culture	____	advanced civilization
5. peer group	____	those of the upper class
6. stereotype	____	common image
7. demography	____	study of land
8. acculturation	____	acquiring language
9. urbanism	____	relates to cities
10. agrarian	____	rural

IV. *Directions:* Write either an original sentence or a definition for each word that clearly demonstrates your mastery of its meanings as used in sociology.

1. **social norms** _____

   _____

2. **mores** _____

   _____

3. **values** _____

   _____

4. **culture** _____

   _____

5. **peer group** _____

   _____

6. **stereotype** _____

   _____

7. **demography** _____

   _____

8. **acculturation** _____

   _____

9. **urbanism** _____

   _____

10. **agrarian** _____

   _____

Sociology

1. **matriarchal family** (mā trē AR kəl)—noun
   A family headed by the mother is a matriarchal family.
   Because my father was frequently absent on business trips, ours was a *matriarchal family*; that is, mother was dominant and made the major family decisions.

2. **patriarchal family** (pā trē AR kəl)—noun
   A family headed by the father is a patriarchal family.
   A *patriarchal family* is most often portrayed in American literature, although the father's role has changed somewhat in recent years.

3. **bureaucracy** (bū ROK rə sē)—noun
   Government structure operated by numerous offices and officials, with clearly defined responsibilities. This structure is often characterized by the following of inflexible rules and the creation of endless red tape.
   The Duncans did not let the irritating *bureaucracy* discourage them from attempting to adopt a child.

4. **utopia** (ū TŌ pē ə)—noun
   Utopia is an imaginary place where everything is perfect.
   Some young people yearn to go to Hollywood because they think this city must be *utopia*.

5. **ethnocentrism** (eth nō SEN triz əm)—noun
   The attitude that one's own race, nation, or culture is superior to all others is called ethnocentrism.
   When people are initially exposed to a different culture, they may fall victim to *ethnocentrism*, a feeling that the new culture is inferior to the one to which they are accustomed.

6. **Malthusian theory** (mal THOO zē ən)—noun

Thomas R. Malthus's (1766–1834) theory that if population is not controlled, it will result in famine, war, and other tragedies.

The *Malthusian theory* was one of the first theories to predict that world hunger would result if population got out of control.

7. **folkways** (FŌK wāz)—noun

Social customs approved by society; but, unlike mores, folkways are not considered morally significant, so they are not strictly enforced.

One of the *folkways* in our society is that a person dress at least fairly formally when attending church, but it is not considered a serious offense if someone shows up wearing jeans.

8. **sanction** (SANK shən)—noun

A sanction is a mechanism of social control for enforcing a society's standards.

After the invasion of Afghanistan, the United States refused to sell the Soviet Union grain; however, this *sanction* proved to be ineffective.

9. **status** (STĀ təs)—noun

Status is a person's social standing in society.

Doctors enjoy a high social *status* in most communities.

10. **ethnic group** (ETH nik)—noun

A group within a society that shares the same traits, such as race, nationality, religion, language, and customs.

Immigrants from Germany were an *ethnic group* that helped to settle Cincinnati, Ohio.

EXERCISES FOR LESSON 36
Sociology

I. *Directions:* Match each definition with the word it defines.

_____ 1. matriarchal family   a. perfect community

_____ 2. patriarchal family   b. customs, but not strictly enforced

_____ 3. bureaucracy   c. mother dominant

_____ 4. utopia   d. a reward or punishment

_____ 5. ethnocentrism   e. organization with rigid rules

_____ 6. Malthusian theory   f. people sharing certain characteristics

_____ 7. folkways   g. father dominant

_____ 8. sanction   h. belief that one's culture is best

_____ 9. status   i. the idea that uncontrolled population leads to serious problems

_____ 10. ethnic group   j. one's position in society

II. *Directions:* In each space, write the appropriate word or words from those listed below.

bureaucracy	matriarchal family
ethnic group	patriarchal family
ethnocentrism	sanction
folkways	status
Malthusian theory	utopia

1. Marybeth was accused of _____ after stating that England's culture is superior to the culture of any other country.

2. People of French descent have been a significant _____ in Maine's history.

3. The newspaper's editor blamed the state _____ for the endless paperwork involved in the proposed construction of a new city bridge.

4. According to the _____, controlled population growth is essential to avoid serious societal problems.

5. Because his father died when Wallis was only two years old, he was raised in a _____.

6. My Aunt Dolores was a part of a _____; her father dominated all family matters.

7. Among the _____ in our society is the expectation that store clerks will be courteous to customers.

8. An example of a reward _____ in the military is promotion to a higher rank.

9. Mr. Porter, a popular coach and biology teacher, enjoys a respected _____ in the community.

10. Maura's idea of _____ is Arizona because of its warm, dry climate and its opportunities for geological exploration.

III. *Directions:* If the words opposite each other in Columns A and B are similar in meaning, write *Yes* in the blank; if they are unrelated, write *No*.

	A		B
1.	matriarchal family	____	family headed by mother
2.	patriarchal family	____	family headed by father
3.	bureaucracy	____	structure with numerous regulations
4.	utopia	____	heaven on earth
5.	ethnocentrism	____	dictator in power
6.	Malthusian theory	____	belief that earth formed ten thousand years ago
7.	folkways	____	traditions expected to be observed
8.	sanction	____	something that tends to reinforce or prohibit certain actions
9.	status	____	penalty for misbehavior
10.	ethnic group	____	individuals in local power

IV. *Directions:* Write either an original sentence or a definition for each word that clearly demonstrates your mastery of its meaning as used in sociology.

1. **matriarchal family** _____

_____

2. **patriarchal family** _____

_____

3. **bureaucracy** _____

_____

4. **utopia** _____

_____

5. **ethnocentrism** _____

_____

6. **Malthusian theory** _____

_____

7. **folkways** _____

_____

8. **sanction** _____

_____

9. **status** _____

_____

10. ethnic group _____

_____

TAKE THE WORD MASTERY TEST FOR SOCIOLOGY.

United States History and Political Science

The United States is a republic, which means that the citizens exercise the powers of government through representatives. To meet this responsibility, citizens need to understand the country's heritage and political system; this is the overriding reason why students are required to study history and government. In this regard, knowledge of the following terms is useful for the study of history and political science.

1. **branches of government**—noun
   The United States federal government is comprised of three branches:

legislative (LEJ is lā tiv)—adjective	Congress, made up of the House of Representatives and the Senate, which makes the laws
executive (ig ZEK yə tiv)—adjective	the president, who enforces the laws
judiciary (joo DISH ē erē)—adjective	the Supreme Court, which interprets the laws

2. **amendment** (ə MEND mənt)—noun
   An amendment is a change or addition to the Constitution, which is the basic document establishing the framework of the federal government. There are currently twenty-six amendments to the Constitution.
   The Thirteenth *Amendment* to the United States Constitution forbids slavery.

3. **Bill of Rights**—noun
   Adopted in 1791 soon after the Constitution went into effect, the first ten amendments to the Constitution are known as the Bill of Rights. It is concerned with such important freedoms as religion and speech.
   Trial by jury is one of the important provisions in the *Bill of Rights*.

4. **checks and balances**—nouns
Rights and procedures in the Constitution that reserve certain privileges to each of the three branches of government and that enable each branch to check, or limit, the powers of the other two.
Among the *checks and balances* existing in our government are the following: Congress (legislative) has the power to remove from office the president and Supreme Court justices; the president (executive) can refuse to sign bills passed by Congress and has the power to appoint Supreme Court justices when vacancies occur; the Supreme Court (judiciary) can declare bills approved by Congress and signed into law by the president unconstitutional.

5. **veto** (VE tō)—noun or verb
The president's refusal or act of refusing to sign a bill into law.
The president said he would *veto* the education bill passed by Congress.

6. **ratification** (rat ə fə KĀ shən)—noun
A power held by a legislative body to approve proposed agreements and amendments.
The Senate's *ratification* is necessary before the treaty becomes official.

7. **boycott** (BOI kot)—noun or verb
An economic means of influencing another nation or business by refusing to purchase its products.
After the British government enacted the Stamp Act, colonial merchants decided to *boycott* English goods, especially tea.

8. **laissez-faire** (les ā FARE)—adjective
An economic policy that opposes government interference in business affairs.
Both presidential candidates stated they favor the *laissez-faire* doctrine for wages and prices.

9. **eminent domain** (EM ə nənt dō MĀN)—noun
The power of the government to acquire private property for public purposes.
The state government's power of *eminent domain* forced the O'Connors to sell a section of their farm so that the highway could be altered.

10. **lobbyist** (LOB bē ist)—noun
A person who represents a special interest group that seeks to influence either the passage or defeat of certain bills.
The *lobbyist* for the oil company appeared before the committee to argue for the bill that would allow new offshore oil drilling.

EXERCISES FOR LESSON 37
United States History and Political Science

I. *Directions:* Match each definition with the word it defines.

_____ 1. branches of government

    a. legislative
power to approve certain
government actions

_____ 2. amendment

    b. first ten amendments to the
Constitution

_____ 3. Bill of Rights

    c. noninterference

_____ 4. checks and balances

    d. legislative, executive, judicial

_____ 5. veto

    e. president's refusal to sign a bill

_____ 6. ratification

    f. representative for a special
concern

_____ 7. boycott

    g. change in the Constitution

_____ 8. laissez-faire

    h. ways government branches can
limit one another

_____ 9. eminent domain

    i. refusal to buy

_____ 10. lobbyist

    j. government's right to secure
private property

II. *Directions:* In each space, write the appropriate word or words from those
listed below.

amendment   branches of government   laissez-faire
Bill of Rights   checks and balances   lobbyist
boycott   eminent domain   ratification
                                                      veto

1. The _____ guarantees numerous personal freedoms.

2. Believing in as few restrictions on business as possible, the president
is encouraging Congress to follow his _____
philosophy.

3. The striking workers are urging people to _____ the company's products.

4. Some historians believe an _____ to the Constitution should be adopted to simplify presidential elections.

5. The president is apparently quite confident that the Senate's _____ of the treaty will occur in two or three days.

6. The governor suggested that the legislature exercise its right of _____ to enlarge the state park near the coast.

7. The three _____ are the legislative, the executive, and the judiciary.

8. The president warned that he would _____ any bills requiring an increase in taxes.

9. Mr. Tapley is a _____ for an environmental organization.

10. The _____ contained in the Constitution are designed to prohibit any branch of government from exceeding its powers.

III. *Directions:* If the words opposite each other in Columns A and B are similar in meaning, write *Yes* in the blank; if they are unrelated, write *No.*

A		B
1. branches of government	____	legislative, executive, treasury
2. amendment	____	addition to or change in the Constitution
3. Bill of Rights	____	first twelve amendments
4. checks and balances	____	economic safeguards
5. veto	____	president's disapproval of a bill
6. ratification	____	presidential appointment
7. boycott	____	refusal to buy
8. laissez-faire	____	economic controls
9. eminent domain	____	power to declare war
10. lobbyist	____	representative for a special group

IV. *Directions:* Write either an original sentence or a definition for each word that clearly demonstrates your mastery of its meaning as used in United States history and political science.

   1. **branches of government** _____

   _____

   2. **amendment** _____

   _____

   3. **Bill of Rights** _____

   _____

   4. **checks and balances** _____

   _____

   5. **veto** _____

   _____

   6. **ratification** _____

   _____

   7. **boycott** _____

   _____

   8. **laissez-faire** _____

   _____

   9. **eminent domain** _____

   _____

   10. **lobbyist** _____

   _____

United States History and Political Science

1. **Manifest Destiny** (MAN ə fest DES tə nē)—noun
   The belief that it was God's will that the United States control the continent, from the Atlantic Ocean to the Pacific Ocean. In the nineteenth century, this doctrine spurred western expansion.
   Manifest Destiny was one of the reasons given for the annexation of Texas.

2. **capitalism** (KAP i tə liz əm)—noun
   An economic system in which businesses are privately owned.
   One of the features of *capitalism* in the United States is that businesses are owned and operated by individuals, not by the government.

3. **communism** (KOM ū niz əm)—noun
   A social system characterized by the absence of classes and common ownership of the means of production and sustenance.
   The Soviet Union's form of *communism* prohibits private ownership of most businesses and property.

4. **socialism** (SŌ shə liz əm)—noun
   An economic system in which the government exercises control over major business enterprises in an attempt to ensure fairness to all members of society.
   An example of Great Britain's *socialism* is its control of medicine by an agency of the national government.

5. **filibuster** (FIL ə bus tər)—noun
   A technique by which a minority of senators attempts to block the passage of a bill through continuous talk, thus delaying the vote.
   The *filibuster* in the Senate has lasted six hours so far.

6. **dark horse**—noun

A long-shot candidate for a party's nomination for an elected office. At the time of nomination, the dark horse is usually the second or third choice; as a result of a deadlock of the other candidates, the dark horse sometimes becomes the party's choice.

In 1860, Abraham Lincoln was a *dark horse* for the Republican presidential nomination.

7. **red herring**—noun

An irrelevant topic that diverts attention from the main issue is called a red herring.

The president angrily remarked that focusing upon his recommendations for welfare cuts was a *red herring* to draw attention away from his balanced budget.

8. **impeachment** (im PĒCH mənt)—noun

The constitutional procedure for removing the president and other high federal officials from office for illegal activities.

President Andrew Johnson, who succeeded the assassinated Lincoln, is the only chief executive to experience *impeachment*, but the final Senate vote was one short of the votes needed to remove him from office.

9. **lame duck**—noun

An elected official whose influence is weakened because he or she is soon to leave office, as a result either of an election defeat or of a law that prohibits another term.

A *lame duck* as a result of losing the fall election, the senator announced that he would be joining a Washington, D.C., law firm.

10. **pacifism** (PAS ə fiz əm)—noun

Pacifism is the opposition to war and physical force as a means of solving conflicts.

Mahatma Gandhi (1869–1948) advocated *pacifism*, and his philosophy of nonviolence influenced Martin Luther King, Jr. (1929–1968).

EXERCISES FOR LESSON 38
United States History and Political Science

I. *Directions:* Match each definition with the word it defines.

_____ **1.** Manifest Destiny

a. method of removing high government officials from office

_____ **2.** capitalism

b. opposition to war

_____ **3.** communism

c. government controls important businesses

_____ **4.** socialism

d. United States' fate to control the continent

_____ **5.** filibuster

e. officeholder whose term is almost over

_____ **6.** dark horse

f. businesses are privately controlled

_____ **7.** red herring

g. something that distracts from the chief issue

_____ **8.** impeachment

h. continuous talk to stop a bill

_____ **9.** lame duck

i. person with only an outside chance to be the party's candidate

_____ **10.** pacifism

j. government control over all economic activities

II. *Directions:* In each space, write the appropriate word or words from those listed below.

capitalism	filibuster	Manifest Destiny
communism	impeachment	pacifism
dark horse	lame duck	red herring
		socialism

1. Most United States citizens strongly oppose _____ as it is practiced in the Soviet Union; it is a system that denies private business enterprise as well as political freedom.

2. The latest newspaper editorial stated that the crime issue was a _____ that blurred the city's major problem, which was an inefficient city administration.

3. The mayor, now a _____, said she would resume her medical practice since the law prevented her from serving a third term.

4. Under _____, people can operate their own businesses.

5. Although not currently the favorite for the nomination, she is considered the _____ of the party.

6. The doctrine of _____ supported the country's westward expansion.

7. The philosophy of _____ was not prominent during World War II as most people supported the war efforts.

8. The senator's _____ lasted nine hours in an effort to delay the vote on the bill.

9. Many people believe that President Nixon would have faced _____ if he hadn't resigned.

10. The government of France operates the nation's transportation and public utilities systems, so _____ exists, but most businesses are operated privately.

III. *Directions:* If the words opposite each other in Columns A and B are similar in meaning, write *Yes* in the blank; if they are unrelated, write *No.*

A		B
1. Manifest Destiny	____	money will be available to pay debts
2. capitalism	____	businesses privately owned
3. communism	____	government controls economy
4. socialism	____	political equality
5. filibuster	____	stalling talk
6. dark horse	____	person with a chance for the nomination but not the favorite
7. red herring	____	smoke screen that keeps attention from the main issue
8. impeachment	____	presidential inauguration
9. lame duck	____	crooked officeholder
10. pacifism	____	belief in expansion to the Pacific Ocean

IV. *Directions:* Write either an original sentence or a definition for each word that clearly demonstrates your mastery of its meaning as used in United States history and political science.

1. **Manifest Destiny** _____

_____

2. **capitalism** _____

_____

3. **communism** _____

_____

4. **socialism** _____

_____

5. **filibuster** _____

_____

6. **dark horse** _____

_____

7. **red herring** _____

_____

8. **impeachment** _____

_____

9. **lame duck** _____

_____

10. pacifism _____

_____

TAKE THE WORD MASTERY TEST FOR UNITED STATES HISTORY
AND POLITICAL SCIENCE.

Business and Economics

A degree in business is the goal of thousands of college students; in addition, thousands of others elect, or are advised to take, a business or economics course so that they can gain insight into the nation's economic system. Learning the terms included in the next two lessons will help you grasp the concepts dealt with in business and economics.

1. **affirmative action** (ə FUR mə tiv AK shən)—noun
   Action designed to increase opportunities for females and minorities through recruitment, training, and promotion so that they are fairly represented in the work force.
   The company has hired many more women and Hispanics in recent years as a result of its *affirmative action* program.

2. **antitrust acts** (AN tē TRUST AKTS)—noun
   Laws designed to prohibit businesses from engaging in exclusive dealing, price fixing, monopolies, and other forms of unfair competition.
   The Federal Trade Commission, referring to the appropriate *antitrust acts*, directed the corporation to reduce its operations in that part of the country so that a more competitive market would be possible.

3. **assets** (AS ets)—noun
   All items of value owned by a person or persons.
   The building, equipment, land, and patents are among the company's *assets*.

4. **balance of trade**—noun
   The term referring to the relationship between a nation's exports (what it sells to other countries) and its imports (what it buys from other countries).
   The United States' *balance of trade* for the past four months indicates that more goods were bought from other countries than were sold abroad.

5. **buyers' market**—noun

A situation in which the supply of goods is greater than the demand for them, giving customers considerable influence over price and terms of sales.

A *buyers' market* enabled us to purchase the appliance for below the advertised price.

6. **cartel** (kar TEL)—noun

An international association of producers of the same product that seeks to obtain monopoly advantages for its members.

Gasoline prices rose sharply in the 1970s because of the *cartel* formed by a number of Middle Eastern countries.

7. **depreciation** (di PRĒ shē Ā shən)—noun

The decline in value of an asset due to usage, age, decay, and other such reasons.

Years of mismanagement resulted in a *depreciation* of the company's manufacturing facilities.

8. **dumping**—noun

Selling products in foreign markets below the prices that these goods are sold for in their home markets.

The International Trade Commission has charged a Far Eastern nation with *dumping* computers in the United States, that is, selling its computers in America at a lower price than they were being sold for in its own country.

9. **entrepreneur** (AN trə prə NUR)—noun

A French term for an individual who develops an enterprise through innovation and risk-taking.

The *entrepreneur* risked a fortune in establishing her unique business, which is now showing an impressive profit.

10. **equity** (EK wə tē)—noun

A firm's net worth; that is, the excess of a firm's assets over its liabilities.

The company has far-flung financial obligations, but its *equity* is still impressive as a result of record-breaking sales.

EXERCISES FOR LESSON 39
Business and Economics

I. *Directions:* Match each definition with the word it defines.

_____ 1. affirmative action

_____ 2. antitrust acts

_____ 3. assets

_____ 4. balance of trade

_____ 5. buyers' market

_____ 6. cartel

_____ 7. depreciation

_____ 8. dumping

_____ 9. entrepreneur

_____ 10. equity

a. an organization formed to establish a business monopoly

b. a bold, daring business person

c. designed to promote career opportunities for females and minorities

d. net worth

e. prohibits monopolies and other types of unfair competition

f. difference between what a country sells and what it buys

g. decline in value

h. a market in which supply is greater than demand

i. selling a product in a foreign market below the price that the product is sold for in its home market

j. cash, goods, and all other things of value

II. *Directions:* In each space, write the appropriate word or words from those listed below.

affirmative action
antitrust acts
assets
balance of trade
buyers' market

cartel
depreciation
dumping
entrepreneur
equity

1. A _____ was formed by the neighboring countries in an attempt to control the price for their iron ore.

2. The representative from the foreign country angrily accused the United States of _____, maintaining that the American transistors being sold in his country were priced significantly lower than they were in the United States.

3. Although a _____ exists, I'm sure Caleb can't buy a new car for the ridiculously low price he has in mind.

4. _____ has been responsible for the significant increase in the number of women admitted to medical schools.

5. The financial analyst was impressed with the firm's _____, pointing out that its assets greatly exceeded its liabilities.

6. Congress enacted a series of _____ in the early part of this century to prohibit monopolies, price fixing, and other unfair business practices.

7. The factory's equipment is becoming worn out, so its loss in value because of _____ is a legitimate tax deduction.

8. Economists are alarmed by the country's _____, saying that export sales are lagging much too far behind import purchases.

9. The young _____, known for her bold initiatives, is once again expanding her business empire.

10. The company's rapid success is remarkable, with _____ now totaling over $750 million.

III. *Directions:* If the words opposite each other in Columns A and B are similar in meaning, write *Yes* in the blank; if they are unrelated, write *No*.

A	B
1. affirmative action	____ measures designed to increase profits
2. antitrust acts	____ laws prohibiting unfair business practices
3. assets	____ valuable possessions
4. balance of trade	____ ratio of imports to exports
5. buyers' market	____ supply of goods greater than their demand
6. cartel	____ net profit
7. depreciation	____ increase in value
8. dumping	____ the discharging of employees
9. entrepreneur	____ bold business person
10. equity	____ strategy for achieving success

IV. *Directions:* Write either an original sentence or definition for each word that clearly demonstrates your mastery of its meaning as used in business and economics.

1. **affirmative action** _____

_____

2. **antitrust acts** _____

_____

3. **assets** _____

_____

4. **balance of trade** _____

_____

5. **buyers' market** _____

_____

6. cartel _____

_____

7. depreciation _____

_____

8. dumping _____

_____

9. entrepreneur _____

_____

10. equity _____

_____

Business and Economics

1. **fiscal** (FIS kəl)—adjective
Pertaining to financial matters.
The company's *fiscal* year begins on July 1.

2. **franchise** (FRAN chīz)—noun
A legal agreement granting an individual or group the right to sell a firm's products or services.
After agreeing to the conditions stipulated, Mr. Striar was granted a *franchise* to operate one of the company's fast-food restaurants.

3. **inflationary** (in FLĀ shə NER ē)—adjective
Pertaining to a substantial rise in prices caused by an excessive expansion of paper money or bank credit.
The union representatives argued that the company's salary offer did not match the rise in the cost of living caused by the prolonged *inflationary* period.

4. **liabilities** (LĪ ə BIL ə tēs)—noun
Debts owed to other firms or persons.
The store owner declared bankruptcy after his *liabilities* continued to exceed his assets.

5. **lien** (LĒN)—noun
The right of a party to the legal possession of property belonging to another party until a debt is paid.
The bank no longer has a *lien* on our house because we recently paid off the mortgage.

6. **recession** (ri SESH ən)—noun
A prolonged economic period in which business is poor and unemployment is high. *Depression* is also a term used to describe such an economic situation.
The economists had predicted a *recession* during the second half of the year, but business and the employment rate continued to be good.

7. **reciprocity** (RES ə PROS i tē)—noun
   A mutual exchange policy in which each party grants the other corresponding commercial privileges.
   The two nations have a policy of *reciprocity*, removing the tariff on certain goods coming from each other's country.

8. **sellers' market**—noun
   A market in which demand is greater than supply, that is, one with more potential customers than there are goods for sale.
   The price of the product has risen sharply because a *sellers' market* exists.

9. **solvency** (SOL vən sē)—noun
   The ability to meet one's debts and obligations.
   The firm's *solvency* enabled the board of directors to pay off all debts and to modernize the plant's equipment.

10. **voucher** (VOU chər)—noun
    A written document, such as a canceled check or a receipt, indicating that a bill has been paid or cash has been received.
    The *voucher* provided evidence that the bill had been paid in full.

EXERCISES FOR LESSON 40
Business and Economics

I. *Directions:* Match each definition with the word it defines.

_____ **1.** fiscal   **a.** demand for a product greater than the supply

_____ **2.** franchise   **b.** pertaining to a significant rise in prices

_____ **3.** inflationary   **c.** economic depression

_____ **4.** liabilities   **d.** legal right to the possession of property belonging to someone else until a debt is paid

_____ **5.** lien   **e.** receipt

_____ **6.** recession   **f.** legal right to sell a firm's products

_____ **7.** reciprocity   **g.** able to pay financial obligations

_____ **8.** sellers' market   **h.** refers to financial concerns

_____ **9.** solvency   **i.** debts

_____ **10.** voucher   **j.** mutual exchange policy

II. *Directions:* In each space, write the appropriate word or words from those listed below.

fiscal	inflationary	lien	reciprocity	solvency
franchise	liabilities	recession	sellers' market	voucher

1. An _____ period is especially hard on people with fixed incomes because the rise in their cost of living is not accompanied by a rise in their incomes.

2. "If you'll scratch my back, then I'll scratch yours" is one way _____ could be defined.

3. Mrs. Righetti politely explained that I would need a receipt or some other type of _____ before she could give me title to the car.

4. Our company is one of the few to use a _____ year of forty-eight weeks in order to have twelve months of four weeks each.

5. Fixed _____ include those debts that must be paid over a long period of time, such as mortgages, bonds, and long-term notes.

6. Clarke has a _____ giving him the exclusive right to sell that company's products.

7. "In the black financially" is one way _____ could be defined.

8. Unemployment rose sharply during the economic _____ of the 1930s.

9. It was a _____ for air conditioners because of the extended heat wave.

10. The judge agreed that the _____ gave the bank the legal right to sell the property.

III. *Directions:* If the words opposite each other in Columns A and B are similar in meaning, write *Yes* in the blank; if they are unrelated, write *No.*

A		B
1. fiscal	____	healthy financial condition
2. franchise	____	legal privilege
3. inflationary	____	downward plunge in prices
4. liabilities	____	debts
5. lien	____	legal hold on property
6. recession	____	depression
7. reciprocity	____	exchange of rights and privileges
8. sellers' market	____	lack of customers
9. solvency	____	sound financial condition
10. voucher	____	tax loophole

IV. *Directions:* Write either an original sentence or definition for each word that clearly demonstrates your mastery of its meaning as used in business and economics.

1. **fiscal** _____

_____

2. **franchise** _____

_____

3. **inflationary** _____

_____

4. **liabilities** _____

_____

5. **lien** _____

_____

6. **recession** _____

_____

7. **reciprocity** _____

_____

8. **sellers' market** _____

_____

9. **solvency** _____

_____

10. **voucher** _____

_____

TAKE THE WORD MASTERY TEST FOR BUSINESS AND ECONOMICS.

Music

The next two lessons are devoted to music and art terms. Not only are fine arts courses personally enriching, but also they deepen our understanding and appreciation of our culture.

1. **a capella** (ak ə PELə)—adjective
   Sung without instrumental accompaniment.
   After the orchestra left the stage, the college choir sang three numbers *a capella*.

2. **adagio** (ə DA zhē o)
   allegro (ə LĀ grō)
   andante (an DAN tä)—adjectives, adverbs, nouns
   Adagio indicates that the music should be performed in a very slow fashion, *allegro* in a lively, fast style, and *andante* in a moderately slow manner.
   The concerto's first movement is played in a spirited *allegro*, the second in a contrasting *adagio*, and the last in a romantic *andante*.

3. <u>**antiphonal**</u> (an TIF ə nəl)—adjective
   Term used to describe alternate or responsive singing by a choir divided into two divisions.
   The choir performed an *antiphonal* composition, with the sopranos and altos chanting in the front of the church and the tenors and basses responding at the back of the church.

4. **aria** (AR ē ə)—noun
   An elaborate melody for a solo voice, with accompaniment, in an opera or oratorio.
   After the tenor sang his *aria*, the audience shouted "Bravo!"

5. **cadenza** (kə DEN zə)—noun
   A short, showy musical passage improvised by a solo instrumentalist.
   The trumpeter demonstrated his creative skill by playing a difficult *cadenza* near the end of the concerto.

6. **crescendo** (kri SHEN dō)
   diminuendo (di MIN yoo EN dō)—adjectives, adverbs, nouns
   Crescendo is a gradual increase in loudness; *diminuendo* is a gradual decrease in loudness or volume.
   The orchestra conductor directed the *crescendo* passages with elaborate arm swings and the *diminuendo* ones with almost imperceptible hand movements.

7. <u>con</u>sonance (KON sə nəns)
   <u>dis</u>sonance (DIS ə nəns)—noun
   Consonance is an agreeable, harmonious mingling of sounds; *dissonance* is a disagreeable, inharmonious mingling of sounds.
   Mozart's name is notable for its pleasant *consonance*; on the other hand, Bartok's music is well known for its harsh *dissonance*.

8. **ensemble** (on SOM bəl)—noun
   A musical group, such as a brass or string quartet, that plays specially arranged compositions.
   The brass *ensemble* was composed of trumpet, trombone, tuba, and French horn players.

9. **forte** (FOR tā)
   pianissimo (pe ə NIS ə MŌ)—adjectives, adverbs, nouns
   Forte indicates that the passage is to be played in a loud, forceful manner, *pianissimo* in a quiet, soft way.
   Be sure to note the dynamics when you play this sonatina, including the *forte* in the first movement and the *pianissimo* in the second.

10. **virtuoso** (VUR choo Ō sō)—noun
    A person who is eminently skilled in music.
    Itzhak Perlman is a violin *virtuoso*.

EXERCISES FOR LESSON 41
Music

I. *Directions:* Match each definition with the word it defines.

_____ 1. a capella		a. to be performed in a moderately slow manner
_____ 2. adagio		b. disagreeable blending of sounds
_____ 3. allegro		c. showy musical passage improvised by a soloist without accompaniment
_____ 4. andante		d. to be played softly
_____ 5. antiphonal		e. musical group
_____ 6. aria		f. gradual decrease in loudness or volume
_____ 7. cadenza		g. outstanding musician
_____ 8. crescendo		h. to be performed in a very slow manner
_____ 9. diminuendo		i. elaborate melody for a solo voice, with accompaniment
_____ 10. consonance		j. agreeable blending of sounds
_____ 11. dissonance		k. gradual increase in loudness or volume
_____ 12. ensemble		l. sung without musical accompaniment
_____ 13. forte		m. to be performed in a lively, fast manner
_____ 14. pianissimo		n. describes alternate, responsive singing by a divided choir
_____ 15. virtuoso		o. to be played loudly

II. *Directions:* In each space, write the appropriate word from those listed below.

a capella   andante   cadenza   diminuendo   forte
adagio   antiphonal   consonance   dissonance   pianissimo
allegro   aria   crescendo   ensemble   virtuoso

1. _____ means a gradual increase in loudness,
   _____ a gradual decrease.

2. Arthur Rubinstein was a piano _____.

3. A string _____, composed principally of violins and cellos, will present an evening concert.

4. _____ is a disturbing mingling of sounds,
   _____ a pleasant blending.

5. An _____ choir sings without instrumental accompaniment.

6. The choirs sang an _____ anthem, with one choir, positioned along one wall of the sanctuary, singing responses to those of the other choir, located along the opposite wall.

7. Near the end of the first movement, the orchestra stopped playing while the pianist improvised a brief but dazzling _____.

8. Musical terms concerned with the rate of speed a passage is played are _____, a very slow rate; _____, a moderately slow rate; and _____, a fast rate.

9. Who was selected to sing the beautiful soprano _____ in the opera *Carmen*?

10. Musical terms concerned with the volume at which a musical passage is played are _____, meaning loud and forceful, and _____, meaning quiet and soft.

III. *Directions:* If the words opposite each other in Columns A and B are similar in meaning, write *Yes* in the blank; if they are related, write *No.*

A	B
1. a capella	____ without voices
2. adagio	____ very slow
3. allegro	____ fast, lively
4. andante	____ unpleasant mingling of sounds
5. antiphonal	____ gradual decrease in volume
6. aria	____ instrumental solo that is improvised
7. cadenza	____ skilled musician
8. crescendo	____ gradual increase in volume
9. diminuendo	____ choir in two divisions that sings alternately
10. consonance	____ harmonious
11. dissonance	____ in a moderately slow manner
12. ensemble	____ musical group
13. forte	____ loud, forceful
14. pianissimo	____ elaborate solo, such as in an opera
15. virtuoso	____ soft, quiet

IV. *Directions:* Write either an original sentence or definition for each word that clearly demonstrates your mastery of its meaning as used in music.

1. a capella _____

_____

2. adagio _____

_____

3. allegro _____

_____

4. andante _____

_____

5. antiphonal _____

_____

6. aria _____

_____

7. cadenza _____

_____

8. crescendo _____

_____

9. diminuendo _____

_____

10. consonance _____

_____

11. dissonance _____

_____

12. ensemble _____

_____

13. forte _____

_____

14. pianissimo _____

_____

15. virtuoso _____

_____

Art

1. **aesthetics** (es THET iks)—noun
   The study of beauty and its meaning, specifically as found in such arts as painting, sculpture, and architecture.
   A course in Renaissance Art deepened my appreciation for *aesthetics.*

2. **avant-garde** (ə vant GARD)—noun, adjective
   An advanced group, especially those in the arts, whose works are considered unorthodox and daring.
   Frank Lloyd Wright and his followers, who rejected the conventional building designs of their day, were among the *avant-garde* of twentieth-century architects.

3. **baroque** (bə RŌK)—adjective, noun
   A style of art characterized by extravagant ornamentation.
   European art in the seventeenth century was in its *baroque* period, that is, in a time when lavish ornamentation was in fashion.

4. **bas-relief** (ba ri LĒF)—noun
   A type of sculpture in which the figures project only slightly from the background.
   The sculpture, depicting a Civil War battle, was in *bas-relief.*

5. **ceramics** (sə RAM iks)—noun
   The art of making objects from clay or similar material.
   Ceramics involves baking pottery and other earthenware at extremely high temperatures.

6. **cubism** (KŪ biz əm)—noun
   A style of art, developed in the early twentieth century, which emphasizes using cubes, cones, and geometric forms instead of representing nature realistically.
   Pablo Picasso helped to popularize the style of *cubism.*

7. **fresco** (FRES kō)—noun, adjective
The art of painting on wet plaster.
Fresco painting requires extraordinary skills because the artist can paint only as long as the plaster remains moist.

8. **impressionism** (im PRESH ə NIZ əm)
realism (RĒ ə LIZ əm)
surrealism (sə RĒ ə LIZ əm)—noun
Impressionism, a style of painting developed in the latter part of the nineteenth century, is characterized by short brush strokes of bright colors used to re-create the impression of light on objects.
Realism is a style of painting that attempts to depict accurately the objects and details in a scene.
Surrealism is a style of painting that attempts to portray what takes place in dreams and in the subconscious mind.
Claude Monet (1840–1926), a master of *impressionism*, focused on light and color rather than on details when he painted a scene. *Impressionism: Sunrise* is the title of one of his earliest landscapes.
Winslow Homer (1836–1910), known for his powerful *realism*, focused on specific details to dramatize the interplay between nature and humans. *The Coming of the Gale* is one of his most famous paintings.
Salvador Dali (1904–1989) is the most prominent artist of *surrealism*. His paintings, often featuring double and repeated images, are concerned with dreams and hallucinations.

9. **kiln** (KIL or KILN)
palette (PAL it)—nouns
A *kiln* is an oven used for baking pottery and other ceramic pieces.
A *palette* is a thin, oval board with a thumb hole at one end; it is used by painters for holding and mixing colors.
The pottery will be baked overnight in the *kiln*.
The artist dabbed a number of brightly colored paints on her *palette*.

10. **lithography** (li THOG rə fē)—noun
The process of producing a figure or an image on a flat, specially prepared stone or metal plate.
Lithography, which produces inked impressions, is one of the most popular graphic arts.

EXERCISES FOR LESSON 42
Art

I. *Directions:* Match each definition with the word it defines.

_____ **1.** aesthetics

a. style of painting concerned with light, bright colors, and the effect the scene made on the artist.

_____ **2.** avant-garde

b. a type of sculpture in which the figures project only slightly from the background.

_____ **3.** baroque

c. an oven

_____ **4.** bas-relief

d. the process of making inked impressions on a stone or metal plate

_____ **5.** ceramics

e. style of art characterized by excessive decoration

_____ **6.** cubism

f. an advanced group, especially in the arts, who are known for starting new trends

_____ **7.** fresco

g. style of painting that attempts to portray dream imagery

_____ **8.** impressionism

h. painting on wet plaster

_____ **9.** kiln

i. board used by artists to hold and mix their paints

_____ **10.** lithography

j. style of painting concerned with the accuracy of details

_____ **11.** palette

k. the making of objects from clay or similar material

_____ **12.** realism

l. study of beauty, particularly as found in art

_____ **13.** surrealism

m. style of art that employs many geometric forms

II. *Directions:* In each space, write the appropriate word from those listed below.

aesthetics   cubism   lithography
avant-garde   fresco   palette
baroque   impressionism   realism
bas-relief   kiln   surrealism
ceramics

1. The silhouettes of the presidents were made by a process known as _____.

2. The artist, a devotee of _____, uses rectangles, triangles, and other geometric forms in his paintings.

3. In the 1920s, the _____ in the movie industry produced a new type of film that was considered quite shocking.

4. The objects that can be made by _____ can range from animal figurines to huge urns.

5. In _____, the artist is concerned more with the interplay of light and colors and the mood it creates than in details.

6. We placed the earthenware mugs in the _____ to bake.

7. Grotesque images and distorted forms characterize _____, a movement in art that has been influenced by Sigmund Freud's emphasis on dreams.

8. _____ architecture, with its elaborate ornamentation, fell out of style by the early 1800s.

9. Travis reportedly mixed a number of paints on his _____ before he was satisfied he had matched the ocean's color.

10. Words such as *authentic*, *preciseness*, and *naturalness* characterize a style of art known as _____.

11. The sculpture on the facade of the bank was in _____, with the numerous figures barely protruding from the wall.

12. Everyone's sense of _____ is awakened when he or she views Michelangelo's *David*, perhaps the world's most beautiful sculpture.

13. Painting on moist plaster, or _____, was popular during the Renaissance.

III. *Directions:* If the words opposite each other in Columns A and B are similar in meaning, write *Yes* in the blank; if they are unrelated, write *No.*

	A		B
	A		**B**
1.	aesthetics	____	concerned with the beautiful
2.	avant-garde	____	old-fashioned artists
3.	baroque	____	lavish decorations
4.	bas-relief	____	small metal sculpture
5.	ceramics	____	making objects from clay
6.	cubism	____	emphasis on geometric forms
7.	fresco	____	painting on wet plaster
8.	impressionism	____	concerned with depicting the mood of the scene rather than the details
9.	kiln	____	oven
10.	lithography	____	process of making linked impressions
11.	palette	____	artist's brush
12.	realism	____	concerned with depicting fantasy
13.	surrealism	____	concerned with depicting the unconscious mind

IV. *Directions:* Write either an original sentence or definition for each word that clearly demonstrates your mastery of its meaning as used in art.

1. **aesthetics** _____

_____

2. **avant-garde** _____

_____

3. **baroque** _____

_____

4. bas-relief _____

_____

5. ceramics _____

_____

6. cubism _____

_____

7. fresco _____

_____

8. impressionism _____

_____

9. kiln _____

_____

10. lithography _____

_____

11. palette _____

_____

12. realism _____

_____

13. surrealism _____

_____

TAKE THE WORD MASTERY TEST FOR MUSIC AND ART.

Biology

Biological (animals, plants) and physical (matter, energy, earth, space) science courses contribute significantly to our understanding of the world. The information that follows is useful for building a solid foundation in the biological and physical sciences.

1. **natural sel<u>ection</u>**—noun
   The belief that in a struggle for existence, the animals and plants of a particular species that survive are those possessing unique adaptive characteristics. This struggle is often called survival of the fittest.
   According to my biology professor, *natural selection*, which involves the concept of survival of the fittest, serves as the foundation of Darwin's theory of evolution.

2. **chromosomes** (KRŌ mə sōms)—noun
   Threadlike bodies in the nucleus of a cell that determine the particular characteristics of an organism; each cell in a human body has 46 chromosomes.
   The majority of animal and plant species have between 10 and 50 *chromosomes* in each cell.

3. **genes** (JĒNS)—noun
   Elements in chromosomes that control the development of hereditary characteristics.
   The color of a dog's coat is determined by *genes*.

4. **Gregor Johann Mendel** (1822–1884)
   Austrian priest whose systematic study of pea plants led him to discover basic principles that govern heredity. Mendel's discoveries are ranked among the greatest in biology.
   Mendel's discovery of the principles of heredity led to the accurate predicting of offspring characteristics.

5. **hybrid** (HĪ brid)—noun or adjective
The offspring of two animals or plants of different species that are crossbred.
The mating of a horse and donkey results in a mule, which is a *hybrid*.

6. **mutation** (mū TĀ shən)—noun
A change in the genes of an organism that is transmitted to the offspring, resulting in offspring differing in some significant way from the parents.
Professor Bailey said that the effects of a *mutation* on the offspring can sometimes be beneficial, but that generally mutation results in harmful abnormalities.

7. **dormant** (DOR mənt)—adjective
Describes an organism that is at rest and not developing.
Seeds will remain *dormant* until the temperature and other environmental conditions are suitable for sprouting.

8. **habitat** (HAB ə tat)—noun
The natural physical area where an animal or a plant lives and thrives.
The *habitat* for seals is the seashore and the sea.

9. **prolific** (prō LIF ik)—adjective
Producing offspring in abundance.
As a result of their frequent litters, rabbits have the reputation of being *prolific* breeders.

10. **transpiration** (tran spə RĀ shən)—noun
Evaporation of water from plants, which mainly occurs through the small holes (stomata) in the leaves of plants.
The action of *transpiration* benefits plants because it increases the amount of water passing up their stems.

EXERCISES FOR LESSON 43
Biology

I. *Directions:* Match each definition with the word it defines.

_____	**1.** natural selection	**a.** describes inactivity
_____	**2.** chromosomes	**b.** discovered laws of heredity
_____	**3.** genes	**c.** theory that organisms best suited survive
_____	**4.** Mendel	**d.** elements in chromosomes that pass on a particular characteristic, such as eye color
_____	**5.** hybrid	**e.** putting forth a large number of offspring
_____	**6.** mutation	**f.** producing abnormality because of a change in a parent's genes
_____	**7.** dormant	**g.** result when two plants or animals of varying species breed
_____	**8.** habitat	**h.** bodies in cells responsible for hereditary characteristics
_____	**9.** prolific	**i.** loss of water vapor by plants
_____	**10.** transpiration	**j.** place where an organism lives and thrives

II. *Directions:* In each space, write the appropriate word or words from those listed below.

chromosomes   Mendel
dormant   mutation
genes   natural selection
habitat   prolific
hybrid   transpiration

1. Much of the feeder corn raised in the Midwest is a _____ developed by crossbreeding different varieties of corn for best characteristics.

2. Evaporation of water from plants is called _____, a process that occurs mainly through the leaves.

3. The effects of a sudden alteration in an organism's genes, called a _____, are unpredictable, but usually the effects are detrimental.

4. Fish are _____ because they produce thousands of eggs, but only a few of the eggs are actually hatched.

5. In winter flower bulbs are _____, but in spring they develop shoots.

6. The hereditary factors that lie within chromosomes are called _____.

7. Organisms that survive a changing environment do so because of advantageous features they possess. This is part of the theory known as _____.

8. Surprisingly, glacial ice is the _____ of some types of bacteria.

9. The experiments of _____ were a great breakthrough for understanding certain laws of heredity.

10. Structures that contain genes, the hereditary units, are _____.

III. *Directions:* If the words opposite each other in Columns A and B are similar in meaning, write *Yes* in the blank; if they are unrelated, write *No.*

	A		B
1.	natural selection	____	freedom of choice
2.	chromosomes	____	precious metals
3.	genes	____	hereditary units
4.	Mendel	____	discoverer of hereditary principles
5.	hybrid	____	crossbred offspring
6.	mutation	____	maturity
7.	dormant	____	active
8.	habitat	____	home
9.	prolific	____	intelligent
10.	transpiration	____	evaporation from plants

IV. *Directions:* Write either an original sentence or a definition for each word that clearly demonstrates your mastery of its meaning as used in biology.

1. natural selection _____

_____

2. chromosomes _____

_____

3. genes _____

_____

4. Mendel _____

_____

5. hybrid _____

_____

6. mutation _____

_____

7. dormant _____

_____

8. habitat _____

_____

9. prolific _____

_____

10. transpiration _____

_____

Biology

1. **plankton** (PLANK tən)—noun
   The microscopic plants and animals that float near the surface in almost all bodies of water.
   An important food source for most fish is the tiny animals and plants, known as *plankton*, that drift in water.

2. **flora, fauna** (FLŌRə, FONə)—nouns
   Flora are the plants, and fauna are the animals of a particular region or period.
   Some citizens are protesting the planned draining of the swamp because they fear that the draining will destroy the *flora* and *fauna*, the plants and animals native to the swamp region.

3. **taxonomy** (tak SON ə mē)—noun
   The science concerned with the describing, naming, and classifying of animals and plants.
   Taxonomy places organisms with similar structures in the same category.

4. **vertebrates, <u>in</u>vertebrates** (VUR tə brātes, in VUR tə brātes)—nouns
   Animals with backbones are vertebrates; animals without backbones are invertebrates.
   Dogs are classified as *vertebrates* because they have a spinal column; worms are classified as *invertebrates* because they have no backbone.

5. **arthropods** (AR thrə pods)—noun
   Invertebrates with a hard outer covering and jointed legs, such as insects.
   Crabs and lobsters are *arthropods* that live in water.

6. **reptiles** (REP tīls)—noun
   Vertebrate animals with horny skins whose offspring are hatched from eggs; all reptiles breathe oxygen, but some live on land and some live in water.
   Examples of *reptiles* are turtles, crocodiles, lizards, and snakes.

267

7. **amphibians** (am FIB ē əns)—noun
Vertebrate animals with moist, smooth skin whose offspring are hatched from eggs; amphibians live partly on land and partly in water.
Toads and frogs are *amphibians*.

8. **mammals** (MAM əls)—noun
Vertebrate animals, including men and women, whose skins are all or practically all covered with hair and whose young are born alive and are fed from mammary glands.
Examples of *mammals* are humans, horses, monkeys, and whales.

9. **hominids** (HOM ə nids)—noun
Hominids include the human family and their ancestors, including extinct humanlike types.
Prehistoric humans are considered *hominids*.

10. **herbivorous** (hur BIV ə rəs),
carnivorous (kar NIV ə rəs),
omnivorous (om NIV ə rəs)—adjectives
Herbivorous describes animals that eat primarily plants; carnivorous describes animals that eat primarily meat; omnivorous describes animals that eat both plants and meat.
Cows are *herbivorous*; wolves are *carnivorous*; humans, because they eat both plants and animals, are *omnivorous*.

EXERCISES FOR LESSON 44
Biology

I. *Directions:* Match each definition with the word it defines.

_____	**1.** plankton	**a.**	eating plants
_____	**2.** flora	**b.**	animals with backbones
_____	**3.** fauna	**c.**	animals with smooth skins that hatch eggs and are at home on land or in water
_____	**4.** taxonomy	**d.**	eating both plants and animals
_____	**5.** vertebrates	**e.**	animals of a specific area or period
_____	**6.** invertebrates	**f.**	animals with horny skins that hatch eggs
_____	**7.** arthropods	**g.**	eating mainly meat
_____	**8.** reptiles	**h.**	plants of a specific area or period
_____	**9.** amphibians	**i.**	animals with hard external covering with jointed legs
_____	**10.** mammals	**j.**	involves the classification of plants and animals
_____	**11.** hominids	**k.**	animals that lack backbones
_____	**12.** herbivorous	**l.**	extremely small animals and plants that live near a water's surface
_____	**13.** carnivorous	**m.**	animals with skins covered with hair and whose young are born alive
_____	**14.** omnivorous	**n.**	humans and their ancestors

II. *Directions:* In each space, write the appropriate word from those listed below.

amphibians herbivorous plankton
arthropods hominids reptiles
carnivorous invertebrates taxonomy
fauna mammals vertebrates
flora omnivorous

1. It surprises many people to learn that whales are vertebrates who are actually _____, as their young are born alive.

2. Snakes are invertebrate animals classified as _____.

3. The classification of organisms based on similar features is the concern of _____.

4. The terms _____ and _____ are used for the plants and animals of a particular region.

5. The primitive Java man is classified with _____ since he is considered a human ancestor.

6. Tiny animals and plants drifting in water are _____.

7. _____ animals are those that eat both meat and plants; _____ animals are those that eat mainly meat, and _____ animals are those that eat plants.

8. Since they have backbones, birds are _____, whereas spiders, lacking backbones, are _____.

9. Frogs are _____ as their natural habitat is both land and water.

10. Centipedes, which have a hard, protective covering and jointed legs, are classified as _____.

III. *Directions:* If the words opposite each other in Columns A and B are similar in meaning, write *Yes* in the blank; if they are unrelated, write *No*.

	A		**B**
1.	plankton	_____	tiny water plants and animals
2.	flora	_____	region's native animals
3.	fauna	_____	region's native plants
4.	taxonomy	_____	dissection of animals
5.	vertebrates	_____	animals with backbones
6.	invertebrates	_____	animals with no spinal columns
7.	arthropods	_____	any four-legged animal
8.	reptiles	_____	invertebrates living in water only
9.	amphibians	_____	vertebrates living on both land and water
10.	mammals	_____	vertebrates whose offspring are born alive
11.	hominids	_____	water organisms
12.	herbivorous	_____	plant-eating
13.	carnivorous	_____	eating both plants and animals
14.	omnivorous	_____	meat-eating

IV. *Directions:* Write either an original sentence or a definition for each word that clearly demonstrates your mastery of its meaning as used in biology.

1. **plankton** _____

_____

2. **flora** _____

_____

3. **fauna** _____

_____

4. taxonomy _____

_____

5. vertebrates _____

_____

6. invertebrates _____

_____

7. arthropods _____

_____

8. reptiles _____

_____

9. amphibians _____

_____

10. mammals _____

_____

11. hominids _____

_____

12. herbivorous _____

_____

13. carnivorous _____

_____

14. omnivorous _____

_____

Biology

1. **homeostasis** (hō mē ō STĀ sis)—noun
   The body's tendency to maintain its internal systems in a normal, stable condition.
   Professor Baxter said that *homeostasis* occurs when we, in an effort to maintain a normal oxygen level, automatically breathe deeply after running.

2. **congenital** (kən JEN i təl)—adjective
   Inborn or existing since one's birth.
   Jeremy says that he's never been able to distinguish certain colors very well; is color blindness a *congenital* condition?

3. **protoplasm** (PRŌ tə plaz əm)—noun
   A chemically complex, colorless, semifluid substance considered the physical basis of life.
   Scientists believe that *protoplasm* is the building block of all animal life.

4. **metabolism** (mə TAB ə liz əm)—noun
   The total chemical and physical processes in the body, including the process by which energy is produced.
   Digestion and respiration activities are involved in *metabolism*.

5. **enzymes** (EN zīms)—noun
   Chemicals, produced by living cells, that participate in many of the body's processes.
   Enzymes in saliva help to break down food in the digestive process.

6. **ossification** (os ə fə KĀ shən)—noun
   Formation and hardening of the bones.
   As people mature, their bones harden, a process called *ossification*.

7. **the body's systems** The seven major systems of the body are:
   digestive (dī JES tiv)—adjective
   Involved in the absorption and elimination of food; includes the mouth, esophagus (tube connecting the mouth to the stomach), stomach, large and small intestines.

respiratory (RES pər ə tōr ē)—adjective
Involved in breathing; includes nose, mouth, trachea (windpipe), and lungs.

reproductive (rē prō DUK tiv)—adjective
Involved in the producing of offspring; includes the ovaries of the female and the testes of the male as well as the other sexual organs.

urinary (YOOR ə ner ē)—adjective
Involved in the elimination of liquid waste; includes the kidneys, bladder, and tubes called ureters and urethra.

circulatory (SUR kə lə tor ē)—adjective
Involved in the transportation of blood throughout the body; includes the heart and blood vessels, such as arteries (carry blood away from the heart), veins (carry blood back to the heart), and capillaries (which connect the arteries and veins).

skeletal (SKEL ə təl)—adjective
Involved in the structure and physical functioning of the body; includes the body's 206 bones and 650 muscles as well as tendons, which are tough cords that attach muscles to bones and to other muscles.

nervous (NUR vəs)—adjective
Involved in the regulation of all the other systems' activities; includes the brain, spinal cord, and nerves.

8. **cardiac** (KAR dē ak)—adjective
Refers to the heart.
Regular exercise strengthens the *cardiac* muscles.

9. **The three major parts of the brain are**
cerebrum (sə RĒ brəm)—noun
Front part of the brain and the largest part; involved in the body's voluntary movements, certain mental actions, stimuli, and impulses.

medulla oblongata (mə DUL ə ob long GA tə)—noun
Lower part of the brain that connects with the spinal cord; involved in the senses of hearing, tasting, and touching as well as heart and breathing actions.

cerebellum (ser ə BEL əm)—noun
Back of the brain; involved in muscle coordination and balance.

10. **dorsal, ventral** (DOR səl, VEN trəl)—adjectives
Dorsal pertains to the back; ventral pertains to the abdomen or the belly.
The *dorsal* region of the body is more rigid than the *ventral* section.

EXERCISES FOR LESSON 45
Biology

I. *Directions:* Match each definition with the word it defines.

_____ 1. homeostasis

_____ 2. congenital

_____ 3. protoplasm

_____ 4. metabolism

_____ 5. enzymes

_____ 6. ossification

_____ 7. body's systems

_____ 8. cardiac

_____ 9. cerebrum

_____ 10. medulla oblongata

_____ 11. cerebellum

_____ 12. dorsal

_____ 13. ventral

a. front and largest part of the brain

b. chemical substances produced by cells

c. refers to the back

d. hardening of the bones

e. part of brain connected with spinal cord

f. semifluid substance that is the basis of life

g. existing since birth

h. refers to the abdomen

i. the sum of the body's chemical and physical actions

j. maintenance of the body's balance internally

k. seven of them, including digestive and circulatory

l. part of the brain involved in coordination and balance

m. pertains to the heart

II. *Directions:* In each space, write the appropriate word or words from those listed below.

body's systems   dorsal   ossification
cardiac   enzymes   protoplasm
cerebellum   homeostasis   ventral
cerebrum   medulla oblongata
congenital   metabolism

1. The _____, connected to the spinal cord, is essential for certain heart and respiration functions as well as for some sense perceptions.

2. The word _____ pertains to the abdomen.

3. The hardening of the bones is called _____.

4. A colorless substance, _____, is the physical basis for life.

5. The total chemical and physical operations of the body, including the production of energy, are involved in _____.

6. _____ is a term referring to the heart.

7. The skeletal and nervous systems are both included in the _____.

8. The _____ is located in the front part of the skull and is the largest part of the brain.

9. A word that refers to the back is _____.

10. _____ is the word used to describe the body's tendency to keep the internal systems in a stable condition.

11. _____ are produced by cells, and they are crucial to many of the body's functions.

12. The _____ is the part of the brain involved in muscle coordination and equilibrium.

13. My veterinarian said my dog has always had a defective heart valve, an unusual _____ condition.

III. *Directions:* If the words opposite each other in Columns A and B are similar in meaning, write *Yes* in the blank; if they are unrelated, write *No*.

A		B
1. homeostasis	____	common infection
2. congenital	____	inborn
3. protoplasm	____	hormones
4. metabolism	____	sum of body's operations
5. enzymes	____	reflexes
6. ossification	____	hardening of bones
7. body's systems	____	skeletal, circulatory, glandular
8. cardiac	____	refers to heart
9. cerebrum	____	back of brain
10. medulla oblongata	____	appendix
11. cerebellum	____	front of brain
12. dorsal	____	back region
13. ventral	____	abdominal area

IV. *Directions:* Write either an original sentence or a definition for each word that clearly demonstrates your mastery of its meaning as used in biology.

1. homeostasis _____

_____

2. congenital _____

_____

3. protoplasm _____

_____

4. metabolism _____

_____

5. enzymes _____

_____

6. ossification _____

_____

7. body's systems _____

_____

8. cardiac _____

_____

9. cerebrum _____

_____

10. medulla oblongata _____

_____

11. cerebellum _____

_____

12. dorsal _____

_____

13. ventral _____

_____

TAKE THE WORD MASTERY TEST FOR BIOLOGY.

Chemistry

1. **catalyst** (KAT ə list)—noun
   A substance that initiates or accelerates a chemical reaction without itself undergoing any permanent change.
   Chlorophyll, a specific protein, has been identified as the *catalyst* responsible for the increased rate at which food is manufactured in plants.

2. **element** (EL ə mənt)—noun
   A fundamental substance that cannot be separated into other substances by chemical means; there are more than a hundred elements.
   Hydrogen is classified as an *element* because it cannot be broken down into other substances.

3. **atom** (AT əm)—noun
   The smallest particle of an element that still has all the chemical properties of the element.
   One oxygen *atom* combines with two hydrogen atoms to form water.

4. **proton, electron, neutron** (PRŌ ton, i LEK tron, NOO tron)—nouns
   A *proton* is a very small particle in all atoms; it has a positive electric charge. An *electron* is a very small particle in all atoms; it has a negative electric charge. A *neutron* is a very small particle in all atoms except hydrogen; it has no electric charge.
   Atoms contain minute particles called *protons*, *electrons*, and *neutrons*.

5. **nucleus** (NOO klē əs)—noun
   The central part, containing protons and neutrons, of an atom.
   The *nucleus* of an atom has a positive charge because of its protons.

6. **compound** (KOM pound)—noun
   A pure substance composed of two or more elements chemically united in a specific proportion; thus, it can be broken down into two or more other pure substances by a chemical change.
   Water is a *compound* whose molecules contain two atoms of hydrogen and one atom of oxygen (H_2O).

7. **molecule** (MOL ə kūl)—noun
   Smallest particle of any material capable of existing independently; it contains all the chemical properties of the material.
   A *molecule* is formed from atoms with balancing attractive forces.

8. **organic, <u>in</u>organic chemistry** (or GAN ik, in or GAN ik)—nouns
   Organic chemistry is concerned with basic substances and matter containing carbon, which include all organisms. *Inorganic chemistry* is concerned with basic substances and matter except for those containing carbon.
   The compounds of plants and animals, which contain carbon, are among the topics studied in *organic chemistry*.
   Acids and minerals containing no carbon are studied in *inorganic chemistry*.

9. **synthesis** (SIN thə sis)—noun
   The process of combining elements to form a compound or of combining simple compounds to form a complex compound.
   The *synthesis* involved in various chemical processes led to the development of manmade materials such as nylon.

10. **solute** (SOL ūt)—noun
    Any gas or solid that will dissolve or disappear when water or other liquid is added.
    Salt is a *solute*; when added to water, the salt disappears.

EXERCISES FOR LESSON 46
Chemistry

I. *Directions:* Match each definition with the word it defines.

_____	**1.** catalyst	**a.** a pure substance containing two or more elements
_____	**2.** element	**b.** atom's central part
_____	**3.** atom	**c.** increases rate of chemical action
_____	**4.** proton	**d.** a fundamental substance that cannot be broken down into other substances
_____	**5.** nucleus	**e.** a solid or gas that dissolves when liquid is added
_____	**6.** compound	**f.** study of materials containing carbon
_____	**7.** molecule	**g.** atomic particle with negative electric charge
_____	**8.** organic chemistry	**h.** atomic particle with no electric charge
_____	**9.** synthesis	**i.** atomic particle with positive electric charge
_____	**10.** solute	**j.** smallest particle of a material that can exist independently and still retain all chemical properties of the material
_____	**11.** electron	**k.** smallest particle of an element
_____	**12.** inorganic chemistry	**l.** combining process
_____	**13.** neutron	**m.** study of noncarbon materials

II. *Directions:*   In each space, write the appropriate word from those listed below.

atom   electron   molecule   organic   solute
catalyst   element   neutron   proton   synthesis
compound   inorganic   nucleus

1. The process of combining elements or compounds is called _____.

2. A substance that increases chemical reaction rate is known as a _____.

3. The study of noncarbon material is included in _____ chemistry.

4. The smallest particle of an element is an _____.

5. Formed from atoms, the smallest particle of a material that can exist independently is a _____.

6. An _____ is a basic substance that cannot be separated into other substances.

7. A _____ is a pure substance composed of united elements.

8. A _____ dissolves when a liquid is added to it.

9. A _____ has no electric charge; a _____ has a positive electrical charge; an _____ has a negative electrical charge.

10. The study of those materials that contain carbon is included in _____ chemistry.

11. The _____ is located in the center of an atom.

III. *Directions:* If the words opposite each other in Columns A and B are similar in meaning, write *Yes* in the blank; if they are unrelated, write *No*.

A		B
1. catalyst	____	something that speeds chemical reaction rate
2. element	____	basic substance
3. atom	____	separating process
4. proton	____	positive electric charge
5. electron	____	negative electric charge
6. neutron	____	no electric charge
7. nucleus	____	atom's center
8. compound	____	substance containing two or more elements
9. molecule	____	measuring device
10. organic	____	contains oxygen
11. inorganic	____	contains no oxygen
12. synthesis	____	combining process
13. solute	____	any liquid

IV. *Directions:* Write either an original sentence or a definition for each word that clearly demonstrates your mastery of its meaning as used in physical science.

1. **catalyst** _____

_____

2. **element** _____

_____

3. **atom** _____

_____

4. proton _____

_____

5. electron _____

_____

6. neutron _____

_____

7. nucleus _____

_____

8. compound _____

_____

9. molecule _____

_____

10. organic chemistry _____

_____

11. inorganic chemistry _____

_____

12. synthesis _____

_____

13. solute _____

_____

Physics

1. **mass**—noun
   The measure of the amount or quantity of a material.
   Any material possesses *mass*.

2. **force**—noun
   A push or pull.
   Water is a common *force*.

3. **work**—noun
   The result of a force moving an object.
   In the language of science, something must be moved before it can be said that *work* has occurred.

4. **energy**—noun
   The ability to do work.
   Electricity and heat can be used to do work, so they are forms of *energy*.

5. **kinetic, potential energy** (kə NET ik, pə TEN shəl)—nouns
   Kinetic energy is energy in motion; *potential energy* is stored energy.
   A swinging hammer displays *kinetic energy*; a resting hammer has *potential energy*.

6. **inertia** (in UR shə)—noun
   The characteristic of an object to resist any change in its motion; that is, the tendency of an object to maintain its condition of rest or movement.
   A force is required to alter an object's *inertia*.

7. **centrifugal, centripetal force** (sen TRIF ə gəl, sen TRIP ə təl)—nouns
Centrifugal refers to the force that propels an object outward from the center of rotation; *centripetal* refers to the force that tends to draw an object inward toward the center of rotation.
When a rock is swung at the end of a string, the rock exerts an outward force on the string as it seeks to fly off in space; this is *centrifugal* force at work. On the other hand, the string pulls inwardly on the moving rock to keep it in its circular path; this is *centripetal* force at work.

8. **hydraulic** (hī DROL ik)—adjective
Describes the use of water or other liquid.
Many machines are operated by *hydraulic*, or liquid, pressure.

9. **oscillate** (OS ə lāt)—verb
To swing to and fro, vibrate, or fluctuate;to make a wave-like motion.
The pendulum will *oscillate* when it is released.

10. **malleable** (MAL ē ə bəl)—adjective
Describes objects that can be hammered or shaped without breaking.
Metals are *malleable*; that is, they can be processed into desired shapes.

EXERCISES FOR LESSON 47
Physics

I. *Directions:* Match each definition with the word it defines.

_____	1. mass	a. to sway in wavelike motion
_____	2. potential energy	b. outward force
_____	3. work	c. using liquid
_____	4. energy	d. quantity of matter
_____	5. kinetic energy	e. pliable, capable of being shaped
_____	6. force	f. push or pull
_____	7. inertia	g. ability to do work
_____	8. centrifugal	h. inward force
_____	9. centripetal	i. force moves an object
_____	10. hydraulic	j. energy in motion
_____	11. oscillate	k. energy that is stored
_____	12. malleable	l. resistance to any change in motion

II. *Directions:* In each space, write the appropriate word from those listed below.

centrifugal	force	kinetic	oscillate
centripetal	hydraulic	malleable	potential
energy	inertia	mass	work

1. The book on the desk will not move on its own accord because of _____.

2. _____ is the ability to do work.

3. Did the lines on the screen _____; that is, did the lines wave back and forth?

4. The amount of a material is defined scientifically as the matter's _____.

5. When an object is rotating, the outward force on the object is called _____ ; the inward force is called _____ .

6. Force must cause movement before it can be said that any _____ has been done.

7. _____ is defined simply as a push or pull.

8. Because steel can be hammered into desired shapes, steel is said to be _____ .

9. Water held in reserve behind a dam is a good example of _____ energy.

10. Water cascading over a dam is an example of _____ energy.

11. The lifts used most frequently in garages to elevate cars are operated in part by _____ power.

III. *Directions:* If the words opposite each other in Columns A and B are similar in meaning, write *Yes* in the blank; if they are unrelated, write *No.*

	A		B
1.	mass	____	diameter
2.	force	____	pull or push
3.	work	____	force that results in movement
4.	energy	____	action
5.	kinetic energy	____	energy in motion
6.	potential energy	____	sun energy
7.	inertia	____	pull toward the earth
8.	centrifugal force	____	outward force
9.	centripetal force	____	inward force
10.	hydraulic	____	automatic
11.	oscillate	____	vibrate
12.	malleable	____	expensive

IV. *Directions:* Write either an original sentence or a definition for each word that clearly demonstrates your mastery of its meaning as used in physical science.

1. mass _____

_____

2. force _____

_____

3. work _____

_____

4. energy _____

_____

5. kinetic energy _____

_____

6. potential energy _____

_____

7. inertia _____

_____

8. centrifugal _____

_____

9. centripetal _____

_____

10. hydraulic _____

_____

11. oscillate _____

_____

12. malleable _____

_____

Astronomy

1. **cosmo<u>logy</u>** (koz MOL ə jē)—noun
   The study of the origin and structure of the universe, which is considered to be space and everything in it.
   The laws that appear to be operating in the universe are among the topics investigated in *cosmology*.

2. **astro<u>nomy</u>** (ə STRON ə mē)—noun
   The study of the planets, moon, sun, and stars; it is concerned with the material universe beyond the earth's atmosphere.
   The distances and sizes of objects in the universe are two of the fascinating subjects studied in *astronomy*.

3. **solar system** (SŌ lər SIS təm)—noun
   Includes the sun, planets, moons, and other matter that revolves around a star.
   Our *solar system* is just one of innumerable solar systems in the universe.

4. **Milky Way**—noun
   One of more than a billion groups of stars called galaxies that exist throughout the universe.
   Our solar system is part of the *Milky Way*.

5. **major planets**—noun
   The major planets of our solar system are Mercury, Venus, Earth, Mars, Jupiter, Saturn, Uranus, Neptune, and Pluto.
   There are nine *major planets* in our solar system.

6. **asteroids** (AS tə roids)—noun
   Sometimes referred to as minor planets, asteroids are solid bodies that orbit between Mars and Jupiter.
   It is possible that *asteroids* are fragmented pieces of a planet that once existed in our solar system.

7. **solar, lunar** (SŌ lər, LOO nər)—adjectives
   Solar refers to the sun; lunar refers to the moon.
   Many houses are being built to take advantage of *solar* energy.
   A full moon to full moon is called a *lunar* month.

8. **zenith, nadir** (ZĒ nith, NĀ dər)—nouns
   The zenith is the highest point in the sky, or the point directly above the observer. The nadir refers to the lowest point, or the point directly beneath a given position.
   The Big Dipper constellation is at its *zenith* this month; in a few months, it will be at its *nadir*, or lowest point.

9. **light-year**—noun
   The distance light travels in a year, which is approximately six trillion miles. (Light travels 186,282 miles per second, so the actual distance in a year is 5.88 million million miles, or 9.46 million million kilometers.)
   Distances in space are so vast that they are calculated in *light-years*. For example, the nearest star to the earth (not counting the sun) is Proxima Centauri, at a distance of 4.3 light-years.

10. **meteorology** (mē tē ə ROL ə jē)—noun
    Meteorology is the science concerned with the atmosphere and its phenomena, including weather and climate.
    Meteorology's main divisions are climate and weather, with climate referring to average weather conditions over a period of years and weather referring to atmospheric conditions at a particular time.

EXERCISES FOR LESSON 48
Astronomy

I. *Directions:* Match each definition with the word it defines.

_____	**1.** cosmology	**a.** pertains to the moon
_____	**2.** astronomy	**b.** our star galaxy
_____	**3.** solar system	**c.** study of the solar system and other matter beyond the earth's atmosphere
_____	**4.** Milky Way	**d.** lowest point
_____	**5.** major planets	**e.** sun, planets, and other matter that revolves around the sun
_____	**6.** asteroids	**f.** nine of them including the earth
_____	**7.** solar	**g.** study of the origin and structure of the universe
_____	**8.** lunar	**h.** solid bodies that orbit between Mars and Jupiter
_____	**9.** zenith	**i.** science dealing with the atmosphere
_____	**10.** nadir	**j.** six trillion miles
_____	**11.** light-year	**k.** highest point
_____	**12.** meteorology	**l.** pertains to the sun

II. *Directions:* In each space, write the appropriate word or words from those listed below.

asteroids	lunar	nadir
astronomy	major planets	solar
cosmology	meteorology	solar system
light-year	Milky Way	zenith

1. The distance of approximately six trillion miles is referred to as a _____.

2. A term that pertains to the sun is _____.

3. The highest point is called the _____.

4. The study of our solar system and other matter beyond the earth's atmosphere is the concern of _____.

5. One of more than a billion groups of stars called galaxies is our _____.

6. A term that pertains to the moon is _____.

7. Climate and weather are the two main divisions of the science of _____.

8. _____ is concerned with the structure and origin of the universe.

9. Mercury, Venus, Earth, Mars, Jupiter, Saturn, Uranus, Neptune, and Pluto are _____.

10. _____ are sometimes called minor planets.

11. The lowest point is called the _____.

12. Our sun and planets are part of our _____.

III. *Directions:* If the word opposite each other in Columns A and B are similar in meaning, write *Yes* in the blank; if they are unrelated, write *No*.

	A		B
1.	cosmology	____	study of earth's interior
2.	astronomy	____	study of matter in universe beyond earth
3.	solar system	____	explanation for universe's origin
4.	Milky Way	____	our galaxy
5.	major planets	____	Mercury, Venus, Earth, Mars, Jupiter, Saturn, Uranus, Neptune, Pluto
6.	asteroids	____	smallest class of stars
7.	solar	____	pertains to sun
8.	lunar	____	pertains to stars
9.	zenith	____	highest point
10.	nadir	____	lowest point
11.	light-year	____	approximately six million miles
12.	meteorology	____	study of meteors

IV. *Directions:* Write either an original sentence or a definition for each word that clearly demonstrates your mastery of its meaning as used in physical science.

1. **cosmology** _____

_____

2. **astronomy** _____

_____

3. **solar system** _____

_____

4. **Milky Way** _____

_____

5. **major planets** _____

_____

6. **asteroids** _____

_____

7. **solar** _____

_____

8. **lunar** _____

_____

9. **zenith** _____

_____

10. **nadir** _____

_____

11. **light-year** _____

_____

12. **meteorology** _____

_____

TAKE THE WORD MASTERY TEST FOR CHEMISTRY, PHYSICS, AND ASTRONOMY.

Computer Science

The widespread adoption of computer science courses into the curriculum on all academic levels has occurred in a remarkably short time. In fact, not only have distinct computer science courses become readily available in recent years, but also such traditional courses as economics and mathematics now require familiarity with computers. It is also true that because of the major impact computers have in many areas of our lives today, computer competency is a graduation requirement at a growing number of colleges. If you are inexperienced with computer terminology, then the following terms will be worthwhile for you to learn.

1. **program**—noun
   An explicit set of instructions for the computer to follow in solving a problem or attaining a certain result.
   This computer *program* enables us to immediately determine our inventory.

2. **character set**—noun
   The letters, symbols, numerals, figures, and punctuation marks used by a particular computer language.
   The decimal digits 0 through 9 and the letters A through Z are included in this computer's *character set*.

3. **data**—noun
   The information given to or produced by the computer.
   The computer provided *data* having to do with industrial production in the southern part of the state for the years 1950–1980.

4. **data base**—noun
   Refers to the computer's ability to perform a variety of operations on a body of data, including filing and retrieval.
   The library's *data base* on my research topic provided me with over twenty helpful sources.

5. **language**—noun

The character set (letters, figures, and so on) and rules a computer must use to operate a particular program.

BASIC, which stands for Beginners All-Purpose Symbolic Instruction Code, is a widely used computer *language*.

6. **binary code** (BĪ nə rē)—noun

A computer code that uses only zeros and ones to represent data.

The *binary code* for this program calls for the letter B to be represented by 01100011.

7. **peripherals** (pə RIF ər əls)—noun

Extra devices, such as printers and data storage components, that can be added to the computer.

One of the *peripherals* you should consider adding to your computer is a letter-quality printer.

8. **terminal**—noun

A peripheral device consisting of a keyboard that enters information into the computer and a screen that displays the computer's responses.

A computer *terminal* combines the features of a typewriter and television screen.

9. **monitor** (MON ə tər)—noun

A video display unit that presents computer characters and other information on a screen.

Although the symbols are quite small, the *monitor* displays them in a vivid fashion.

10. **CPU (Central Processing Unit)**—noun

The CPU controls the computer's operations; it is the "heart" of the computer.

The *CPU* is the part of the computer that follows a program's instructions.

EXERCISES FOR LESSON 49
Computer Science

I. *Directions:* Match each definition with the word it defines.

_____ **1.** program

a. functions done on a body of data to obtain certain results; compared to a filing system

_____ **2.** character set

b. devices added

_____ **3.** data

c. information provided or produced

_____ **4.** data base

d. keyboard with printer or screen

_____ **5.** language

e. essential unit for regulating activities; the heart of the computer

_____ **6.** binary code

f. the letters and other symbols used

_____ **7.** peripherals

g. use of 0 and 1

_____ **8.** terminal

h. computer's set of instructions

_____ **9.** monitor

i. symbols and rules used for a particular program

_____ **10.** CPU

j. display screen

II. *Directions:* In each space, write the appropriate word or words from those listed below.

| binary code | CPU | data base | monitor | program |
| character set | data | language | peripherals | terminal |

1. BASIC is the _____ of many computer programs because its words and figures are easily understood.

2. The key part of the computer that processes the words and numbers is the _____ .

3. A code that uses only zeros and ones to represent its information is called a _____ code.

4. The information is displayed on the _____.

5. The set of instructions used to achieve a particular result is referred to as a _____.

6. A piece of equipment that includes a keyboard and screen is known as a _____.

7. _____ is the general name for the information the computer processes.

8. Storage and printing components are extra devices referred to as _____.

9. Punctuation marks are part of the _____ of computers.

10. A substitute for a filing system, _____ usually refers to the set of programs available to manipulate the data.

III. *Directions:* If the words opposite each other in Columns A and B are similar in meaning, write *Yes* in the blank; if they are unrelated, write *No*.

	A		B
1.	program	____	set of instructions
2.	character set	____	letters, figures
3.	data	____	information processed or produced
4.	data base	____	keyboard
5.	language	____	results
6.	binary code	____	0 and 1
7.	peripherals	____	additional equipment
8.	terminal	____	end of program
9.	monitor	____	screen
10.	CPU	____	Controlled Program United

IV. *Directions:* Write either an original sentence or a definition for each word that clearly demonstrates your mastery of its meaning as used in computer science.

1. **program** _____

   _____

2. **character set** _____

   _____

3. **data** _____

   _____

4. **data base** _____

   _____

5. **language** _____

   _____

6. **binary code** _____

   _____

7. **peripherals** _____

   _____

8. **terminal** _____

   _____

9. **monitor** _____

   _____

10. **CPU** _____

    _____

Computer Science

1. **cassette**—noun
   A cassette is a device for storing information, which is done by converting data to audio signals on magnetic tape.

2. **disk**—noun
   A disk is a flat, record-shaped object that is magnetically coated so that it can store electronic data.
   Although both *cassettes* and *disks* can store computer data, the disk is more convenient because information can be retrieved from it faster.

3. **modem** (MŌ dem)—noun
   A modem is a device that is used to link a computer to a telephone system, permitting information to be transmitted from one computer system to another.
   A *modem* permits us to transmit data to our company's main computer in California.

4. **bit**—noun
   A bit is the smallest piece of information stored in a computer.
   The term *bit* refers to *binary digit*.

5. **byte** (BĪT)—noun
   A byte usually consists of eight bits that are considered as a single unit.
   A *bit* is either 0 or 1; a *byte* is a made-up word or character that represents specific information.

6. **compatible** (kəm PAT ə bəl)—adjective
   This term is used when the software (programs) and/or the hardware (physical equipment) can be exchanged between computer systems.
   I will have to buy some additional equipment to make my home computer *compatible* with the one I use at my office.

7. **protocol** (PRŌ tǝ kol)—noun

This term refers to the precise set of rules that describe how to do particular computer operations.

This booklet contains the *protocol* that must be followed to send information between two computers.

8. **volatile** (VOL ǝ til)—adjective

This term describes data that are lost when the computer's power is turned off.

The memory that is inside the main part of the computer is *volatile*, so I am storing this valuable information on a disk.

9. **documentation** (dok ū men TĀ shǝn)—noun

Documentation refers to the written support material that describes the specifications of a computer or explains the operations of a program.

I will have to study the *documentation* for this program to see if it is capable of performing the statistical calculations I need.

10. **chip**—noun

A chip is a tiny silicon wafer used to make electronic memories and circuits.

A *chip* the size of a postage stamp may have as many as thirty thousand electronic parts.

EXERCISES FOR LESSON 50
Computer Science

I. *Directions:* Match each definition with the word it defines.

_____ **1.** cassette   **a.** a computer's smallest piece of information

_____ **2.** disk   **b.** written support material

_____ **3.** modem   **c.** rules describing specific computer operations

_____ **4.** bit   **d.** means that a program or equipment of different computer systems can be exchanged

_____ **5.** byte   **e.** device that permits data transmissions over telephone lines

_____ **6.** compatible   **f.** stores information as sounds

_____ **7.** protocol   **g.** small silicon wafer

_____ **8.** volatile   **h.** eight bits

_____ **9.** documentation   **i.** describes data that are lost when the computer is turned off

_____ **10.** chip   **j.** flat, record-shaped object used for storing information

II. *Directions:* In each space, write the appropriate word from the list below.

bit	compatible	protocol
byte	disk	volatile
cassette	documentation	
chip	modem	

1. A _____ is a device that enables computer information to be transmitted over telephone wires.

2. The tiny wafer used in computer electronic circuits is called a _____.

3. He told me the memory inside the main part of the computer is _____, so don't turn off the computer until you've taken steps to save your work.

4. Used for storing computer information, a _____ looks like a record.

5. The written material, or _____, clearly explains this computer's capabilities.

6. A _____ is a unit of information consisting of eight bits.

7. The tape of the _____ stores the computer data as audio sounds.

8. _____ refers to the sequence of steps that must be followed to do specific computer operations.

9. The word _____, which comes from the term *binary digit*, is the smallest piece of information in a computer.

10. These microcomputers are quite different from one another, so their programs are not _____.

III. *Directions:* If the words opposite each other in Columns A and B are similar in meaning, write *Yes* in the blank; if they are unrelated, write *No*.

A	B
1. cassette	____ stores computer information on tape
2. disk	____ record-shaped object used to store computer data
3. modem	____ device enabling the transmission of data over telephone wires
4. bit	____ wafer containing electronic circuit
5. byte	____ memory unit in the computer
6. compatible	____ exchangeable
7. protocol	____ rules to follow
8. volatile	____ data that are safely stored
9. documentation	____ collection of valid data
10. chip	____ smallest piece of information in a computer

IV. *Directions:* Write either an original sentence or a definition for each word that clearly demonstrates your mastery of its meaning as used in computer science.

1. cassette _____

_____

2. disk _____

_____

3. modem _____

_____

4. bit _____

_____

5. byte _____

_____

6. compatible _____

_____

7. protocol _____

_____

8. volatile _____

_____

9. documentation _____

_____

10. chip _____

_____

TAKE THE WORD MASTERY TEST FOR COMPUTER SCIENCE.

TAKE THE WORD MASTERY TEST FOR THE ENTIRE TEXT.

Appendix A: Parts of Speech

1. ADJECTIVES

An **adjective** describes or modifies a noun or pronoun.

> Did you see that gray cat?
>
> Two cars were parked in the driveway.
>
> He is tall, dark, and handsome.

Specific suffixes are associated with adjectives, including -able, -ible, -al, -ful, -ous, -ive, and -y:

> She is a capable worker.
>
> This is a reversible coat.
>
> We celebrated the national holiday in Alaska.
>
> Martin is a careful driver.
>
> They own a spacious ranch in Wyoming.
>
> The plaintiff is suing for punitive damages as well.
>
> Sharon is cleaning her messy room.

Demonstrative adjectives: these people, this office

Descriptive adjectives: lovely day, pale color

Interrogative adjectives: What program? Whose coat?

Limiting adjectives: three children, several cars

Possessive adjectives: our apartment, my uncle

Proper adjectives: American flag, Canadian imports

2. ADVERBS

An **adverb** describes or modifies a verb, adjective, or another adverb.

> modifying a verb: Brittany walked quickly to the door.

> modifying an adjective: She was extremely happy to get the news.

> modifying another adverb: Time went by very slowly.

Adverbs often indicate when, where, how, and to what extent.

> when: The Artesonis will arrive tomorrow.

> where: Steve, place the chair here.

> how: The children sang loudly.

> to what extent: We were completely bewildered by the news.

Adverbs often end in the suffix -ly, as a number of preceding examples illustrate.

3. CONJUNCTIONS

A **conjunction** is a word used to join words or groups of words. There are coordinating, subordinating, adverbial, and correlative conjunctions:

Coordinating conjunctions: and, but, for, nor, or, yet, so

> Rain and fog made driving difficult.

> We had the day off, but Sheila had to work.

> My husband bought a ticket, for he loves that type of music.

> Meredith couldn't answer the question, nor could I.

> You can have ice cream or pudding for dessert.

> Shane had his car repaired, yet it is still giving him trouble.

> We were tired, so we didn't attend the ceremony.

Subordinating conjunctions: after, although, because, if, etc.

> After they left, the party broke up.

> Although it was cloudy, Sandy still got a sunburn.

> He refused dessert because he is on a diet.

> The game will be played next week if it has to be canceled today.

Adverbial conjunctions: consequently, however, therefore, etc.

> Bob never heard from him again; <u>consequently</u>, he rented the apartment to someone else.

> I knew that he had applied for that position; <u>however</u>, I was surprised that he got it.

> Our plane leaves at 6:30 A.M.; <u>therefore</u>, we will have to get up early.

Correlative conjunctions: either–or, neither–nor, not only–but also

> I think that <u>either</u> the cat <u>or</u> the dog broke the lamp.

> It is clear that <u>neither</u> the owners <u>nor</u> the workers want the strike to continue.

> We were <u>not only</u> surprised <u>but also</u> embarrassed by the news.

4. INTERJECTIONS

An **interjection** is a word or phrase that expresses strong emotion.

> <u>Ouch</u>! I've been stung by a bee.

> <u>Look out</u>! There's ice on the sidewalk.

5. NOUNS

A **noun** is a person, place, or thing.

> person: Emily

> place: Prince Edward Island

> thing: wrench

Common nouns refer to general classes: woman, city, building

Proper nouns refer to people, places, or things: Anne, Detroit, Empire State Building

Collective nouns name groups: family, team, class

Concrete nouns name tangible things: rock, flower, table

Abstract nouns name intangible things: idea, bravery, democracy

6. PREPOSITIONS

A **preposition** is a word that combines with a noun or pronoun to form a phrase; prepositional phrases generally serve as adjectives or adverbs.

Laura mowed the grass [after lunch.]——prepositional phrase
preposition   noun

We have full confidence [in him.]——prepositional phrase
preposition   pronoun

These words often function as prepositions:

above	behind	during	from	of	to
before	by	for	in	over	with

7. PRONOUNS

A **pronoun** is a word used in place of a noun.

noun: <u>Pablo</u> is coming home tomorrow.

pronoun: <u>He</u> is coming home tomorrow.

These words are among those that serve as pronouns:

I	he	it	they	themselves	which	there	anybody
you	she	we	myself	who	what	those	somebody

8. VERBS

A **verb** is a word or group of words expressing action or the state of being of a subject.

action verb: Yolanda <u>laughed</u>.

state of being verb: Our guests <u>are</u> here.

A **transitive verb** expresses action that has an object:

verb   object
↓   ↓
Ilse set the package on the table.

verb   object
↓   ↓

Omar <u>flipped</u> the <u>pages</u> of the telephone directory.

An **intransitive verb** does not have an object.

verb
↓

The boy <u>shivered</u>.

verb
↓

The ice and snow <u>melted</u>.

A **linking verb** connects the subject and a complement that renames or describes the subject:

Jamie <u>is</u> the captain.

The clothes <u>seemed</u> inexpensive.

An **auxiliary** or **helping verb** combines with other verbs to form phrases.

helping verb
↓

Katherine <u>can paint</u>.

helping verb
↓

The windows <u>were closed</u>.

These words function as auxiliary or helping verbs.

am	been	can	did	does	has	is	might	shall	was
are	being	could	do	had	have	may	must	should	were

Appendix B: Using the Dictionary

A dictionary is the best source for learning the precise meanings of words; moreover, it provides other valuable information about words, including their pronunciation, spelling, part of speech, and origin.

Printed below is the entry for *demagogue* found in the *Random House Dictionary of the English Language*.* By becoming familiar with key parts that have been identified and explained, you will be able to take better advantage of the information a dictionary provides.

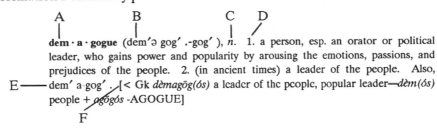

A. The **entry word** is printed in boldface type and divided into syllables.

B. The **pronunciation** of the word is shown in parentheses, with the pronunciation indicated by specific letters, lines, and symbols. A guide to the pronunciation is generally found in the inside cover of a college dictionary as well as at the bottom of every other page.

C. The **part of speech** of a word is indicated by an abbreviation; parts of speech are commonly abbreviated in this manner:

adj.—adjective   prep.—preposition
adv.—adverb   pron.—pronoun
conj.—conjunction   v.—verb
inter.—interjection   v.i.—verb intransitive
n.—noun   v.t.—verb transitive

(See Appendix A for a review of the parts of speech.)

---

* *The Random House Dictionary of the English Language, College Edition* (New York: Random House, Inc., 1968), p. 352.

D. The word's **definition**; many words have more than one definition, making it necessary to select the one that is appropriate to the context in which the word is being used. (In the example, two definitions for *demagogue* are listed.)

E. A **variant** of the word's spelling, *demagog*. (Variants are words with more than one acceptable spelling, such as *theater* and *theatre*.) The first spelling listed, *demagogue*, is the more common or preferred spelling.

F. The **etymology** of the word is enclosed in brackets. (Etymology is concerned with the origin and history of words.) The following are the most common abbreviations used to indicate the language from which a word originated:

OE—the language spoken in England from the years 700 to 1100
ME—the language spoken in England from 1100 to 1500
OF—the language spoken in France from 800 to 1200
F—the language spoken in France today
L—Latin, spoken by the Romans approximately 2000 years ago
GK—Ancient Greek, spoken in Greece approximately 2500 years ago

(Our example indicates that *demagogue* came from the Ancient Greek language and that it meant "a leader of the people, popular leader.")

Most college dictionaries also include numerous supplemental pages devoted to a variety of topics like the following:

- directions for using the dictionary
- pronunciation guide and other explanatory notes
- directories and tables of useful information
- basic manual on grammar, punctuation, and style
- brief history of the English language

The following dictionaries are among those recommended for college students:

> *The American Heritage Dictionary*
> *The Random House College Dictionary*
> *The Random House Dictionary of the English Language*
> *Webster's Ninth New Collegiate Dictionary*
> *Webster's II New Riverside University Dictionary*

Note: Be sure to use the guide words when looking up a word in a dictionary. **Guide words** are those words printed in boldface type at the top of each page indicating the first and last words printed on that particular page. Because words in a dictionary are listed in alphabetical order, the guide words reveal whether or not the word you are looking for can be found on that particular page. (In our preceding example, the guide words *delineative* and *demand* indicated that *demagogue* would be found on that page.)

Appendix C: Science Word Parts

Although you may have previously studied some of the following word parts, they are worth reviewing and others are worth learning. All of them can contribute to your understanding of numerous words used in the biological and physical sciences.

1. **anthropo-** pertains to the human race
    Anthropology involves the study of the origins, beliefs, and cultural development of humankind.

2. **geo-** refers to the earth
    Geography involves the study of the earth's surface, climate, population, and natural resources.

3. **zoo-** refers to animals as opposed to humankind
    Zoology is the branch of biology that deals with animals.

4. **hemi-, semi-** half
    The southern *hemisphere* includes the half of the earth between the South Pole and the equator.
    A *semispheric* object is shaped like half a sphere.

5. **hydro-** pertains to water
    Hydrology is concerned with the distribution and properties of water of the earth and the earth's atmosphere.

6. **mega-** large, great; million, multiplied by one million
    A *megaton* bomb is equal to the explosive force of one million tons of TNT.

7. **trans-** across
    Transitory means passing by or temporary; the larval stage of insects is a *transitory* state.

8. **thermo-** refers to heat
    Thermodynamics is concerned with the relationships between heat and the mechanical energy of work.

9. **astro-** star
    An *astronaut* is one who travels in space.

10. **iso-** equal

   Isobars are lines drawn on weather maps to connect points that have equal barometric (atmospheric) pressure.

11. **hyper-** over, above, excess

   Laboratory tests are being performed to find the cause of the water's *hyperacidity.*

12. **hypo-** less, under, insufficient

   A *hypodermic* needle is a needle that is inserted under the skin.

13. **-itis** inflammation, such as redness, swelling, pain

   Bronchitis is inflammation of the tubes leading to the lungs.

14. **bi-** two

   The *bicuspid* teeth have two distinct points.

15. **poly-** many

   A *polymorphous* animal or plant is one that has passed through many stages or forms, such as a butterfly.

16. **neuro-** nerve

   The branch of medicine concerned with nerves and the nervous system is *neurology.*

17. **anti-** against or opposite

   An *anticorrosive* is a substance that prevents or counteracts rusting or deterioration.

18. **-dermis** skin

   The outer layer of human skin is called the *epidermis.*

19. **hemo-** blood

   The protein matter of the red blood cells that carries oxygen throughout the body is called *hemoglobin.*

20. **micro-** small

   Microbes are small organisms that cannot be seen without the aid of a *microscope.*

Index of Word Parts (Section One)

Index of General Words (Section Two)

Index of Academic Terms (Section Three)

diminuendo, 250
disk, 303
dissonance, 250
documentation, 304
dormant, 262
dorsal, 274
dumping, 238

earth, 291
electron, 279
element, 279
eminent domain, 226
empirical, 202
energy, 285
ensemble, 250
entrepreneur, 238
enzymes, 273
equity, 238
ethnic group, 220
ethnocentrism, 219
executive, 225
experimental group, 202
exposition, 196
extrinsic motivation, 207

fauna, 267
figures of speech, 190
filibuster, 231
fiscal, 243
flora, 267
folkways, 220
force, 285
forte, 250
franchise, 243
free association, 208
fresco, 256

genes, 261
genre, 189

habitat, 262
herbivorous, 268
homeostasis, 273
hominids, 268
hybrid, 262
hydraulic, 286
hyperbole, 195

impeachment, 232
impressionism, 256
inertia, 285
inflationary, 243
inorganic, 280
intrinsic motivation, 207
invertebrates, 267

judicial, 225
Jupiter, 291

kiln, 256
kinetic energy, 285

laissez-faire, 226
lame duck, 232
language, 298
legislative, 225
liabilities, 243
lien, 243
light-year, 292
literal, 189
lithography, 256
lobbyist, 226
lunar, 292

major planets, 291
malleable, 286
Malthusian theory, 220
mammals, 268
Manifest Destiny, 231
Mars, 291
mass, 285
matriarchal family, 219
medulla oblongata, 274
Mendel, Gregor Johann, 261
Mercury, 291
metabolism, 273
metaphor, 190
meteorology, 292
Milky Way, 291
modem, 303
molecule, 280
monitor, 298
mores, 213
motor skills, 201
mutation, 262